# GATEWAY TO OBLIVION

# GATEWAY TO OBLIVION:

## The Great Lakes' Bermuda Triangle

## HUGH F. COCHRANE

55145

JUN 24 '80

DOUBLEDAY CANADA LIMITED, TORONTO, CANADA

DOUBLEDAY & COMPANY, INC., GARDEN CITY, NEW YORK

1980

ISBN: 0-385-15376-7
Library of Congress Catalog Card Number: 79-7597
Copyright © 1980 by Hugh F. Cochrane
Printed in the United States of America
First Edition

*This book is dedicated to my mother,*
*to Jeanie G. Thorogood, and to those*
*individuals who feel there are still*
*dimensions and energies beyond those*
*known to science.*

# Acknowledgments

Grateful acknowledgment is made to the following for their contributions:

Robert E. Ater, Malva Dee, Thomas Edward Ross, John Brent Musgrave, Harry Belfrage Picken, B.Sc., Jim Bryers, Norman Weis, Murray Martin, Mrs. George Wheeler, Mary E. Smith, Zachary G. Space, Sylvia J. Laidler, Gene Duplantier, Malcolm Williams, Tom Grey, Mary Margret Fuller, Jay Gourley, Harry Tokarz, and Robert Spec.

Also: Dodd Mead & Company, De Vorss & Co. Inc., Madoc *Review*, the Church of Jesus Christ of Latter-Day Saints, the Picton *Gazette*, Ontario Historical Society, the Canadian Department of National Defence, and the United States Coast Guard.

# Contents

It is a strange place where ships, planes, and people vanish into thin air, where weird fogs and globes of light abound, where ominous waters shroud sinister events. It is a place where eerie negative emissions have gripped psychics and bizarre UFO events astound researchers. It is an enigma with a two-hundred-year history of disasters that have drained insurance companies of millions of dollars in claims and set records for mysterious events that pale the famed Bermuda Triangle. Ship losses alone number in the thousands. Yet authorities refuse to discuss the matter openly.

And where is this realm of suspended reality? It is not in a remote corner of the earth. It is located right in the middle of the North American heartland, the region known as the Great Lakes!

# 1 The *Bavaria* Is Missing

Near the end of a cool May, in 1889, several tall-masted ships sailed out of Kingston harbor, at the eastern end of Lake Ontario, to search for a missing vessel. There had been a storm over the lake. Not uncommon in these waters. And the *Bavaria*, the missing ship, had failed to make port.

Her absence had raised concern among the ship's owners and relatives of the crewmen. There was good reason for this concern, for, although Lake Ontario is not the largest in the Great Lakes chain, it has one rather weird, if not deadly, anomaly that none of the others possess. It has the Marysburgh Vortex. This vortex, like the famed Bermuda Triangle, is a swathe of water in the eastern end of the lake that has a long history of bizarre circumstances that have caused the loss of numerous ships and their crews. According to marine insurance records, the Great Lakes have a higher concentration of shipping accidents than any comparable area elsewhere. And it has held this unenviable position for over a hundred years.

But the problem doesn't end there. In its variety of mysterious events this region outranks anything found in the Bermuda Triangle, the Hoodoo Sea, or any of the other so-called zones of mystery in other parts of the world.

More important, this end of Lake Ontario appears to be the focus of an unknown, invisible vortex of forces that not only erupts intermittently throughout these waters but, at times, spews out an invisible cloak to encompass and cause disasters in other parts of the Great Lakes, the regions surrounding them, and even the skies above.

With this in mind, it was an act of courage that led the captain and crew of one of the rescue vessels, the *Armenia*, to sail directly into these waters to search for the missing ship *Bavaria*.

When the *Armenia* was nine miles south of the Main Duck Islands and well inside this zone of mystery, her crew sighted the *Bavaria* sitting upright and grounded on a small desolate shoal known as Galloo Island. This discovery sent a feeling of relief rippling through the crew of the *Armenia* and her captain ordered his ship to sail closer to the stranded vessel. When they were within hailing distance, the crew of the *Armenia* called out, but there was no reply to their eager shouts, no figures appeared on the deck. The only sound that came from the strangely silent ship was the uneasy creaking of her timbers as the long swells from the lake nudged her to and fro, swaying her masts like giant crosses.

A dark frown clouded the face of the *Armenia*'s captain as he and a few of his crew rowed across and boarded the *Bavaria*. From the time they stepped aboard, they sensed something drastically wrong. And after they had searched the ship from end to end, their suspicions were confirmed. There was absolutely no trace of the *Bavaria*'s crew. The empty vessel gave up only strange clues to an even deeper mystery, one that has confounded investigators of Great Lakes mysteries to this day.

Among the discoveries made aboard the Bavaria was that, aside from a small amount of water in her hold, the ship was completely seaworthy. In fact she was sailed back to Kingston once she had been freed from the shoal. There was certainly nothing wrong with the vessel that would cause her crew to abandon her. Nor was there a single clue to show where the crew had gone.

In the captain's cabin they found all his papers and a box containing a large sum of money collected from cargo that had been delivered to American ports. In the galley oven they found a batch of freshly baked bread. But the strangest of all was a small repair job lying on the deck. It was only a minor repair job and it appeared to have been set aside momentarily when the seaman had been interrupted in his work, intending to return. But for some reason he never came back to finish the task. He, along with the captain and the rest of the crew, had vanished from the Bavaria and none was ever seen again. The only living thing on the ship was a canary that still chirped in its cage in one of the cabins.

The captain and the crew of the Armenia left Galloo Island to report their find, pondering the puzzle of why all aboard the Bavaria had left a perfectly seaworthy ship. Where had they gone that money and food no longer had any value? The bread in the oven, the money, the important papers, and the small unfinished task on the deck were evidence that the departure of the captain and crew had been sudden. But why?

When the Armenia reached port and the news of the discovery was announced, the circumstances found aboard the Bavaria set off wild speculation. It also reopened old questions of what had become of others that had sailed out across these strange waters and had never been seen or heard from again. It raised questions of other dark mysteries that have plagued this region of the continent since earliest times.

While this speculation raged, others less imaginative remained silent, expecting that at least one of the crew of the *Bavaria* would turn up to tell his tale of ordeal on the lake. But as time passed, it became obvious to all that not even the bodies of the captain or crew would return to shore. They had all mysteriously vanished as if whisked from the face of the earth. They were victims of the Marysburgh Vortex.

Even before the discovery of the *Bavaria* and the unexplained fate of her crew, investigators had tried unsuccessfully to solve the riddle of this enigma of Lake Ontario. In the end they all failed.

In the case of the *Bavaria*, some investigators claimed that the evidence found aboard the ship pointed to something bizarre and unnatural that had overtaken the vessel. Some believed that an invisible force had invaded the ship and had driven all aboard her insane, causing them to seek an escape, even suicide.

The fact that her single lifeboat was missing led others to conclude that the captain and crew had succeeded in escaping from the ship. But this did not explain what had happened to them or why they needed to abandon their vessel since it was seaworthy.

Others suggested that those aboard the *Bavaria* were the victims of the storm, that they believed the ship was sinking and abandoned her. If so, what about the money and papers left in the captain's cabin? Also, what about the bread in the galley oven and the unfinished repair job? These are not the sorts of tasks seamen engage in during a storm that threatens to sink their ship.

Considering this evidence, it would seem that the *Bavaria* had weathered the storm and that things had returned to normal and regular duties were being attended to. Then something out of the ordinary occurred on board the ship. Whatever it was, that something was so threatening and vehement that all of those aboard attempted to flee the vessel, possibly in the single lifeboat. But none escaped whatever horror it was that had invaded their ship. In the end it claimed them all.

There are some final and confusing facts surrounding this story of the *Bavaria*. A few days after she had been found sitting aground on Galloo Shoal, a strange report came to light. The captain of another vessel, which had been in the same area as the *Bavaria* during the storm, told how his crew had sighted a lifeboat on the lake with two motionless figures at the oars. The captain had made repeated attempts to get his ship close enough to rescue the two men, but each attempt had been frustrated as the lifeboat was drawn away. No matter how he maneuvered the vessel, the lifeboat was impossible to reach. In the end the rescuers had to give up in defeat and stand by helplessly as the lifeboat disappeared into a thick fog and was never seen again.

At no time during the rescue attempt did the two men at the oars make any effort to save themselves. Instead, they sat as if hypnotized, staring blankly as each attempt failed. When last seen they were sitting immobile at the oars as they were drawn to their doom.

Around the same time a lighthouse keeper in the same area reported that he, too, had tried to rescue two men in a lifeboat but had failed each time he almost had them in his grasp. He also claimed that the men had made no effort to assist in their own rescue.

Almost a hundred years have passed since this strange fate

overtook the *Bavaria* and her crew. Those who have tried to puzzle out these mysterious events have come no closer to the solution than did the stunned seamen who witnessed the event or examined the clues at firsthand.

While the mystery surrounding the *Bavaria* may have stunned many at the time, it was by no means an isolated incident in this region. Six years earlier, one fall morning in 1883, the vessel *Quinlan* had sailed out of Oswego harbor on the south side of Lake Ontario with a full load of coal for delivery to the north shore. The route her captain had chosen was a direct line across the lake, one that would take her right through the middle of the Marysburgh Vortex. The ship never completed the voyage. Those who witnessed the violent events and survived to tell the tale revealed that the eastern end of the lake was inhabited by unknown forces—forces that still inhabit the region today.

The first sign that the *Quinlan* was destined for a bizarre fate occurred shortly after the vessel had cleared the American shore and sailed into a fog bank. Such conditions are not too unusual in these waters during the late fall. But the seamen themselves admitted that this was an unusually thick fog, which shrouded the vessel in a wet gray blanket. With this came a rapid drop in temperature and snow crystals began to form, quickly coating the decks and hatches with a thick layer of white. The snow accumulated with unbelievable rapidity and the crew went to work with shovels to clear the ship of the burden that was making her top-heavy. Although the crew struggled frantically to get rid of the mounting snow, there seemed to be no end to the strange fall. As fast as it was removed, more piled up.

As it turned out, this was to be the least of the problems that plagued the crew of the *Quinlan*. Waves began to rise

around the vessel and their battering became a savage fury
few had ever witnessed. The exhausted crew were forced to
abandon their efforts to save the ship. All they could do was
to cling tightly to railings or riggings to keep from being
swept overboard as the ship was tossed up and down and
from side to side.

Thunderous waves continued to smash her hull and drive
her on before the fury of the storm, and there was no telling
in which direction the *Quinlan* was headed, for her compass
had suddenly ceased to function, its needle turning lazily in
its case. But even with it, navigation would have been impossible. The vessel was now under the control of other forces,
which refused to release their grip. Lashed from all directions,
the ship plummeted on, her route totally out of the control of
human hands. Not knowing where they were going or what
the final outcome would be, the crew could only cling desper-
ately and pray.

Shortly before noon the *Quinlan* slammed into the Marysburgh shore. Her masts had been snapped off, and her hull
was split as violent waves pounded her to pieces on the rocks.
Powerless to stop the destruction, the crew hung on to what
was left of the ship while witnesses gathered on the shore
frantically trying to rescue the exhausted seamen from the
wreckage. They managed to reach only a few; the rest were
sucked from the tangled mass of timbers and rigging and
pulled into the lake that had just cast them out. They were
never seen again.

The few who survived were carried to nearby homes and
given the warmth and care they had never expected to experience again. When they were finally able to tell their story
they all agreed on one thing: The ship had been gripped by
"some odd attraction!"

Since that time no one has ever been able to discover just what that "odd attraction" was or what caused it to grip the *Quinlan*. The same applies to the "frost fogs" or whatever strange force made the compass useless. It is only now that researchers and investigators are beginning to discover the extent of the domain of these forces.

In recent times there have been others who have encountered strange fogs in this region of the continent, and they have fared no better than the seamen of early times. In 1966, an experienced pilot was flying his light aircraft on a well-established route along the south shore of Lake Erie, southwest of Lake Ontario, when he encountered a fog that enveloped his plane and blotted out all visual contact with the earth. Within minutes he was isolated in a white sea of nothingness, unable to tell up from down. He shouted into his microphone to the stunned controllers at the Cleveland Air Traffic Control Center, saying that he did not know what was the matter, that he was spinning, that he was falling. His radio transmission ended abruptly at the same time that his blip disappeared from the radar screens of the Cleveland Air Traffic Control.

The United States Coast Guard launched an immediate search over the land and water in the area where the plane was last reported. The search lasted several days but not a trace of the missing aircraft was ever found. It had entered the fog and had silently passed into oblivion.

According to the Toronto newspapers, visibility was poor on November 8, 1977, when Tom Walker, a veteran pilot with nine years' flying experience, took off from Toronto's Island Airport for a flight to his home at Owen Sound, a short eighty miles north of Lake Ontario. Walker never arrived. Two days later he was found hobbling down a main highway in a well-settled area just outside metropolitan Toronto and was rushed to a local hospital. After being treated for a broken ankle and multiple injuries, he told his wife that the last thing he remembered was flying into a cloud or fog. He had no idea where he was when he was found on the highway, nor could he tell where his aircraft was located.

While this was going on in the hospital, Canadian Government search and rescue investigators were in communication with the relatives of two other men whose aircraft had failed to reach the airport at Maple, just north of Toronto, after a flight from the head of the lakes. No trace had been found of this pair or their aircraft and the missing men's relatives had employed a psychic to aid in the search. After weeks of fruitless searching and with costs totaling thousands of dollars, the search was abandoned. No trace was ever found of the missing men and their aircraft.

The strange forces at work in this part of the continent are no different from the forces at work in the other zones of mystery around the world. It would seem natural to expect the authorities in government or science to demonstrate an interest in these mysteries and set about trying to determine their true cause. Not so. Throughout the history of the Marysburgh Vortex and the Bermuda Triangle, next to nothing has been done to initiate a thorough study of the phenomena encountered here. As a result, these areas have become the domain of the Fortean writers and investigators who reveal the mysteries but never arrive at a final solution.

An example of one of the oddities that might have a bearing on the unexplained events occurring in the Lake Ontario region is the number of magnetic anomalies found here. There are no fewer than fourteen of these magnetic anomalies—areas of strong local magnetic disturbance—plainly marked on present-day navigation charts issued for Lake Ontario. The majority of these locations are clustered in the eastern end of the lake. If these are no more than strong local magnetic disturbances, then at best they could only cause a careless navigator to sail off course.

The question is, Do these anomalies represent something else? Possibly a source of undiscovered forces emerging from the earth? Whatever it is, *something* in the eastern end of Lake Ontario is reaping a harvest of destruction. According to Willis Metcalfe in his book, *Canvas & Steam on Quinte Waters*, two thirds of all shipping losses in this part of the Great Lakes occurs in the eastern end of Lake Ontario. In 1883, for example, forty vessels and 672 lives were lost in Lake Ontario, the greater majority in the eastern end!

In 1950, in a joint venture between the United States Navy and the Canadian National Research Council, a study was begun on magnetic anomalies and other such phenomena. As part of this project, surveys were made around Lake Ontario. This led to further investigations by a Canadian team of scientists under Wilbert B. Smith of the Canadian Department of Transport. During their investigations they uncovered some strange facts. They discovered areas of "reduced binding" in the atmosphere near the shore of the lake. In one report these areas were described as pillar-like columns—some almost a thousand feet across and reaching thousands of feet up into the atmosphere—which were invisible and detectable only by sensitive equipment. Inside these columns some peculiarities were noted in gravity and magnetism and what appeared to be a reduction in the nuclear binding forces holding matter together. It was also discovered that some of these "columns" were mobile and never remained in one location for any length of time. Such an unusual discovery should have created some interest within the scientific community. Evidently it did not. Investigations of these areas were dropped and nothing further on the subject has been released.

For the present there is no way of determining whether one of these zones of reduced binding—a sort of gravity or magnetic hole—had anything to do with the sudden disappearance of the ship *Picton* as she approached the Marysburgh Vortex in 1900. But whatever it was that caused this vessel to vanish made it look as if the vessel had sailed into another dimension. And it happened in front of a number of astounded witnesses!

There were two vessels following along behind the *Picton* on that clear June morning as she sailed toward the Marysburgh Vortex. The ships *Minnes* and the *Acacia* had both left port with the *Picton* and they had her in plain sight. If she had struck something and sunk they would have had time to see what was wrong and rush to her aid. But there was no such preliminary warning. One minute the *Picton* was there and the next she was gone. It was as quick as that, according to the witnesses.

At first the crews of the *Minnes* and *Acacia* did not believe their eyes and scanned the surface of the lake before the shock of what had happened gripped them. Then they quickly offered prayers to heaven and sailed directly into the area where the *Picton* had been seen minutes before. For the next few hours the two ships crisscrossed the area while their crews hung over the rails, their faces grim as they searched the water for some trace of the people or the wreckage that they were certain should be there. But they might as well have saved themselves the trouble. There was no trace of the vanished *Picton* then or after.

An uncomfortable mood came over the crews of both ships

as they finally abandoned the search and resumed their course to the northeast. When they reached port on the Canadian shore and told of the almost impossible event that they had just witnessed, the news was received with skepticism and disbelief. After the initial shock had passed, word was spread to other ports around the lake and a watch was kept for evidence that might surface with the passage of time. It was a slim chance, but there was not much else that could be done.

As among all seafaring people, speculation grew among the lakeshore inhabitants, but none of the proposed theories helped to solve the sudden disappearance of this vessel. Nor was the saga of the *Picton* about to fade away. Several days after the event, at Sackets Harbor, a few miles northeast of the point where the ship vanished, another strange chapter unfolded that was destined to make the mystery even deeper.

In this small port a fisherman's son had watched a bottle float in and out of the harbor repeatedly over a period of two days. His curiosity aroused, the boy borrowed his father's skiff and rowed out to retrieve the bottle. Inside the bottle he found a note from Captain Jack Sidley, master of the *Picton*.

News of the discovery spread around the lake like wildfire. Relatives identified the handwriting as Captain Sidley's, but there was more to the find than just the note. When the bottle was found, it had been tightly stoppered and its top fastened with wire! Also, in Sidley's last communication with the outside world he had written that he had lashed himself to his son so that they would both be found together.

These two facts make it clear that, although the *Picton* had abruptly vanished, its captain was very much alive for some time after the event. He certainly would not have written such a note before the event occurred. So where was the captain when he wrote the note?

Historians and researchers have spent many hours trying to puzzle this one out and have got nowhere. The clues seem to defy solution. Most have agreed that if the ship had instantly sunk to the bottom of the lake without leaving a trace of material evidence to float over the spot and mark the location for the searchers, then Captain Sidley certainly had no time to write a note, much less find a bottle to put it in and a piece of wire to secure the top. Having done all this, he then had to find a piece of rope to tie himself to his son.

The note suggests that the captain knew he did not have long to live. From this we can assume that he had found himself in a hostile environment from which he saw no escape. This might suggest that he was trapped inside his ship on the bottom of the lake. The cargo of coal that the *Picton* was carrying would have been sufficient to take the ship to the bottom if the hold had somehow filled with water. At this location the lake slopes sharply from two hundred feet to a depth of five hundred feet—enough to cause the trapped air to burst the hull and send debris to the surface along with a foaming fountain of air and water. But searchers who had remained in the area for several hours stated they had found nothing.

In an effort to provide a solution to this mystery, present-day writers have suggested that, like other zones of mystery around the world, the Marysburgh Vortex harbors a doorway into another dimension, an invisible gateway into some realm outside our reality. As bizarre as this sounds, it is certainly no more so than the instant disappearance of the *Picton*.

Further, if there is such a doorway to a mysterious realm, then it operates only intermittently, because right after the *Picton* had vanished, both the *Minnes* and the *Acacia* sailed directly into the same area and neither of them were suddenly transported out of this world.

If nothing else, the sudden disappearance of the *Picton* appears to offer evidence of forces on this earth that can cause a vessel and its crew to vanish without a trace. Such evidence could put a rip in the curtain of reality created by a science whose laws do not allow for such an event.

Ever since Vincent Gaddis wrote his original article in 1964, bringing public attention to the Bermuda Triangle and the mysterious events occurring there, many other writers have probed this enigma of the Atlantic. Countless books and articles have been written on the subject, adding to the unexplained things that have taken place in that region of the Atlantic over the years.

All of this, rather than uncovering a final solution, has only deepened the mystery even further. None of these writers or curious investigators has succeeded in finding the root cause. Nor can they agree as to what form that solution might take.

Among the speculated causes of these strange occurrences are suggestions that the Bermuda Triangle is under the control of UFO entities—aliens from another planet who have turned the area into a base of operations for their excursions to this planet: sort of a way station for intergalactic explorers. Part of those operations includes the gathering of specimens of ships, planes, and people for a galactic museum.

If this is true, then there must be a magnificent museum somewhere out in the universe filled with the hundreds of ships, planes, and humans who have vanished in this area over the centuries.

Other writers and reporters investigating these events attribute the cause of the mystery to strange rays of energy being generated and beamed to the surface by a huge crystal column on the ocean floor, said to be a relic of an ancient civilization of Atlanteans who used the crystal as a power source.

This column, topped with a specially faceted cap to collect the sun's energy, was said to have been used by the ancient Atlanteans to power their ships, submarines, and aircraft. It was also supposed to be capable of emitting rays that helped cure ailments of the Atlanteans. It is believed to have been originally located in one of their temples, and this, along with the continent these people inhabited, sank to the bottom of the Atlantic thousands of years ago when earthquakes and other disturbances shattered the earth and brought about massive geographical changes.

The temple and its crystal are said to now lie beneath the ocean intact at the southern corner of the Bermuda Triangle, with the crystal still blasting its energies up from the depths.

This solution, though unique, seems improbable because the amount of sunlight penetrating to the bottom of the ocean is rather small, therefore the energies produced by such a mechanism would tend to be weak. Furthermore, according to the records, most of the strange events occurring here take place during the night hours or during periods when thick fog blankets the area, and at these times the sunlight would not be available to power the crystal device.

However, whether or not this region of the Atlantic is a "twilight zone" haunted by intergalactic specimen collectors or a region being swept by an ancient laser gun that has run amuck makes little difference. It is still a fact that the so-called Bermuda Triangle is a region of dark mystery that will not be solved or go away because of bland indifference on the part of established science and high officialdom.

The Bermuda Triangle is by no means the only such region on this earth. In 1972, Ivan T. Sanderson set about to examine and record many of the other zones around the world. These also were areas where things go missing in strange circumstances. His research brought to light many other little-known triangles of mystery scattered across the globe, some located hundreds of miles from any water.

All told, Sanderson pinpointed twelve such areas and found them to be equally spaced and so located that they form a geodesic grid when connected by lines drawn on a map of the world. Each intersection of this grid, be it over land or water, marks a location where mysterious events have been recorded and for which no explanation can be found. In other words, each intersection of the grid marks the location of a zone of mystery rivaling the famed Bermuda Triangle.

While researching material for historical articles on the Great Lakes region I noticed a similarity between many of the strange events that occurred in this region and those which Vincent Gaddis and others turned up. When I re-examined some of these events, and others dating back to the earliest recorded times, I discovered that many of them fell into the same unexplained category that characterizes other such zones on the earth.

But something more important began to emerge from this research, something that was lacking in all the other zones of mystery. This was the strong evidence that zeroed in on the eastern end of Lake Ontario as the focus for the mysterious forces at work in this region of the continent.

In an article for Marty Singer of *Saga* magazine, in November 1975, I outlined some of the strange events that have plagued this region over the years and pinpointed the Marysburgh area as the center of activity. Since that time, further research has revealed other unexplained events in that area that are even more puzzling than anything encountered in the Bermuda Triangle.

Further, these other events indicate a wider spectrum of

mystery, which now appears to have its roots in the strange forces and energies erupting from the earth in this area. At times these forces expand outward to include other portions of the Great Lakes chain, even erupting into the skies above them or the lands bordering these waters.

Amazingly, the power appears to stem from clusters of invisible volcano-like fountains that spiral up from activity taking place deep in the earth. While these eruptions seem to be electrical in nature, they are not listed in any scientific text. Yet they seem to have been known to the priests and leaders of ancient civilizations. Also, if we are to believe the ancient writings and the evidence coming to light today, these forces and energies can affect not only material matter but also the human mind!

In the area of the Marysburgh Vortex, the shores of Lake Ontario narrow in toward the St. Lawrence River, creating a funnel-like enclosure. Through this the waters gathered from the expanse of the 300,000-square-mile Great Lakes Watershed must flow. Geographically and geologically this region is a strange mixture of curious features. It sits on the edge of the Precambrian shield and has been subjected to volcanic and seismic events that have left it a topographical oddity rounded off by glacial activity in the past. Its shores are rugged, knifed by bays and coves, its surface dotted with islands, reefs, and shoals, its bottom shattered by silt-filled fissures and faults.

This area also takes in the deepest point in the lake—an icy well of blackness almost 850 feet deep, from which nothing returns. Into this the lake bottom plunges with a roller-coaster suddenness.

Like inland waters in any other part of the world, navigation here calls for a certain amount of caution. This is where the shores narrow in toward Wolfe Island; navigation here can be a mariner's nightmare. As one seaman put it, "This end of the lake can be a one-way ticket to oblivion!"

Both the United States and Canada share this expanse of water, just as they share the unexplained events that occur in this area. Yet government authorities on both sides of the border view these mysteries as wordplay and imagination. They are quick to point out the records, which show that many ships have passed through this region and, at worst, have suffered only minor damage from storms.

All this is true. Many have passed through this zone of mystery without any lasting effects. However, when the toll of losses is examined and the common accidents and the usual mishaps due to foul weather are accounted for, there remains a number of "accidents" for which no logical explanation exists. And the reason for this is simple enough: The forces causing these unexplained "accidents" are beyond present-day understanding. They are forces which have never been explored scientifically.

As the next chapters will reveal, these unknown forces have been erupting in and around this region for centuries and they have been ignored for far too long.

They cannot be ignored any longer!

# 2 The Mystery Deepens

It is a recorded fact that the captain and crew of the ten-thousand-ton Greek freighter *Protostatis* were experienced seamen. They were well acquainted with foreign ports and hazardous waters. They had weathered many ocean storms, but these in no way prepared them for what they encountered in Lake Ontario.

It was late in September 1965, when the *Protostatis* made ready to sail from Detroit. That was when it was discovered that two crewmen had jumped ship. It is not known whether the men had any premonition of the fate that awaited their vessel, but the ship sailed without them.

Her course lay down the center of Lake Erie and Lake Ontario, down the St. Lawrence, and out to sea. Along the way they had to pass right through the Marysburgh Vortex.

The *Protostatis* never reached the sea.

As this ship knifed her way into the eastern end of Lake Ontario she was pursued by ominous black clouds that followed the ship like a pall of doom. It was to be a storm that none aboard the *Protostatis* would forget in a hurry.

By the time the ship had reached her rendezvous with the vortex, she was being battered by mountainous waves that rose with a fury and slammed the ship from end to end. With each mighty jolt her hull heaved and strained until one after the other her steel plates began to buckle and it seemed as if she was about to burst inward. As seams sprang open under the onslaught, the ship began to take on water and her crew fought to keep her afloat. But it was a losing battle. They were fighting more than a storm. They were fighting forces that appeared intent on the destruction of the vessel!

On the bridge with the captain were two Great Lakes pilots, men well trained in the ways of the lakes, who knew the shoals, the reefs, the tricky currents.

Or so they thought.

Before the storm ended, the ship was miles off her course. She was not sailing up the lake, she was heading directly for the shore and she plowed into the rocks on Travis Shoal.

None seemed sure what had caused this "accident." Nor was there time to argue the point. The ship was in serious condition. When tugs arrived to try to free her, it was discovered that two more of her crew had gone missing. Now the vessel was shorthanded.

With over one hundred of her steel plates buckled, her pumps had to be run at full pressure to keep her afloat while the tugs brought her limping into Kingston harbor. However, there was no dry dock large enough to accommodate a ship the size of the *Protostatis*. She would have to go on to Montreal. In order to hold her together until she got there, concrete was poured and packed into her weakened structure.

But the relative safety of the St. Lawrence River was still

five miles away and she might just as well have tried to go to the moon. No sooner was she out of Kingston harbor than she wound up off course again! She swept over the Quebec Head buoy and rammed hard into Wolfe Island.

Seaway authorities were stunned and began to wonder what had taken possession of the *Protostatis*. In all his years of service the captain of the ship had never encountered anything like it. Certainly with two skilled Seaway pilots on board nothing like this should have happened.

According to the captain, the *Protostatis* was in strange waters and in the control of a strange master!

Strange master indeed, for now her electrical power unaccountably failed, her engines stopped, and the ship was dead in the water. Then a dispute broke out and the tugs, instead of staying with the stricken vessel, immediately left the scene.

No one could decide what had caused the two groundings, or what to do to save the stricken vessel. At this point the Canadian federal authorities stepped in and the inquiries to sort out the problems and determine the legal responsibilities were conducted behind closed doors.

To oldtime lake seamen it seemed obvious that an outside force was bent on claiming her. With the *Protostatis* powerless, the captain had no means of escaping whatever it was that was wrecking his ship. Forced into a decision that no captain cares to make, he, along with what was left of his crew, abandoned the ship and left the country.

Under a Canadian court order, the RCMP and the Canadian Coast Guard moved in and took charge of the ship. Two tugs, a freighter, and a derrick scow approached the vessel along with a small army of forty-five men whose objective was to get the ship off the rocks and tow her to safety as quickly as possible. But as soon as the ship was freed, the whole armada ended up seeking shelter when a storm threatened to wrest the reclaimed vessel from their grasp.

Now they gave up any hope of getting the *Protostatis* to Montreal for repairs. Instead, the badly weakened ship was taken in the opposite direction, out of the vortex the way she had entered. It was hauled to Toronto, 130 miles to the west. Its destination, the scrap heap.

As mentioned earlier, those who discovered the areas of reduced binding—a weakening of the nuclear forces holding matter together—also discovered that at times this strange anomaly was mobile, wandering about rather than fixed in one place for any length of time. While the majority of mysterious events has historically remained localized in the Marysburgh Vortex, there are times when this phenomenon also shifts its domain of destruction to other lakes in this chain, to the lands around them, and also into the skies.

On a clear fall day in September 1960, two CF-100 jets of the Canadian Armed Forces streaked across the sky near the north shore of Lake Ontario. Their mission was routine and the trailing jet had the lead jet in sight as they arrowed through some wispy clouds. Suddenly the lead jet vanished from the sky!

The stunned pilot in the other aircraft stiffened at the controls, unable to believe what had happened. He quickly scanned the sky all around, above and below. There was nothing. He called his base for confirmation and was told he was alone in the sky. They, too, had seen the blip of the jet disappear from their radar screens.

Certain that something mechanical had gone wrong with the other plane, the pilot circled back, searching for a billowing parachute or a plume of smoke to mark the location where the jet had plunged down. He found nothing. The only clue to show that there had been another aircraft in the sky with him was the contrail of the missing jet. The trail dead-ended abruptly at the point where the jet had vanished.

On notification, search and rescue teams immediately began a search of the surrounding area. Farmers and residents were questioned and the area was crisscrossed. But there were no witnesses to any crash, and no wreckage.

On the chance that the jet might have glided out over the lake, the searchers shifted their attention to the water. In this area of the lake and within ten miles of the shore the greatest depth is under two hundred feet, most of it less than a hundred. This is shallow enough for any aircraft the size of a CF-100 to be easily spotted. But there was no oil slick or debris visible, and no traces of this aircraft were ever found.

In similar cases of disappearances in the Bermuda Triangle, the search and rescue authorities there are quick to point out that the Gulf Stream is capable of carrying off wreckage or oil slick. Sometimes these will turn up hundreds of miles away. This makes the task of locating the remains of ships and planes that much more difficult. But in Lake Ontario there are no such currents. Those that are present in this lake are sluggish and mild. Anything the size and weight of an aircraft, particularly a CF-100 interceptor, would have sufficient weight to anchor itself on the bottom and remain there.

According to the accident report filed by the Canadian Defence Department, this missing aircraft, number 18469, was not found at the bottom of Lake Ontario or any other place.

With no evidence to evaluate, the investigators of this strange "accident" had no alternative but to close the file on the case. As is the practice with accidents involving military

aircraft of the Canadian Forces, this file was stamped SE-
CRET. The information on this case was released on a personal request to the Directorate of Information Services of
the National Defence Headquarters. This file shows that the
whereabouts of the missing jet and its pilot is unknown to the
defense authorities.

When material objects vanish without a trace, as in this
case, the way is open for speculations and theories about
doorways into other dimensions. If there are such doorways,
then they must also exist in the sky!

When an aircraft vanishes, there is no evidence to examine.
But sometimes, even with evidence, an event remains unex-
plainable.

This was the case with an aircraft "accident" in 1963 involving a private aircraft, CF-LVJ, on a sightseeing trip over
Niagara Falls at the western end of Lake Ontario. Almost
half of the plane's left wing was sheared off in midair and the
plane went into a spin that slammed it into the earth, killing
the pilot and his passengers.

Crash investigators who examined the wreckage were puzzled by the fact that the sheared-off portion of the wing was
never found while the remainder of the wing and parts of the
cabin were found strewn along the flight path. From laboratory analysis of the remaining portion of the wing, investigators were able to determine that it had been structurally
sound before the accident. The wing had not broken at the
point of the shearing due to metal fatigue or any other such
cause. It appeared to have been sheared off as if the wing had
made contact with an invisible wall or force while the aircraft
was in flight.

The crash investigators made tests to determine if there
were any unusual air currents in the area where the accident

occurred. Weather reports were double-checked, and witnesses who had seen the accident were questioned closely. None of this diligent investigation turned up any clue as to what the aircraft had hit in midair. As a result, the case was officially closed and the file was stamped "cause undetermined."

That was not the end of the invisible something lurking in the skies over this part of the continent. In September 1970, a similar "accident" occurred farther north in this same area of Lake Ontario. Again it involved a private aircraft, CF-OUR, which seems to have encountered an invisible wall or force which again sheared away ten feet of the plane's right wing. The aircraft spun to the ground and crashed, killing the pilot and three passengers.

CF-OUR's accident file is also stamped "cause undetermined."

While some aircraft in this region encounter invisible objects or forces, others appear to drop into a well and are sucked straight down in a vertical plunge into the earth.

On August 10, 1977, two CF-5 jets of the Canadian Armed Forces were speeding across the sky near the eastern end of Lake Ontario. Suddenly, for no apparent reason, one of the jets went into a vertical dive at high speed. The plane was demolished in the crash, killing the pilot.

Later, the pilot of the remaining jet reported that, before the erratic maneuver, there had been no hint of any problem being experienced by the other pilot. There was nothing to indicate that he had attempted to use his radio to report any malfunction, nor had he used his ejection system to escape from the plunging aircraft.

This was the second Armed Forces jet to be destroyed in this manner in less than three months. Crash investigators were unable to determine why these jets had gone into a sudden dive or why the pilots had not corrected the erratic maneuver or tried to escape certain death by ejecting.

In May 1971, a light aircraft took off from an airport near Lake Scugog just north of Lake Ontario. After beginning a normal flight the aircraft was observed, by witnesses on the ground, to fly in a downward spiral until it plowed into the earth. All aboard were killed. Investigators examined what was left of this aircraft, CF-CVU, but were unable to discover what had caused the crash.

Again, the accident was labeled "cause undetermined."

Many such air crashes—well over a hundred similar to those listed here—have found their way into the accident files of the American and Canadian governments. These are air crashes from one particular region: areas around Lake Ontario or the Great Lakes!

Why should so many unexplained accidents involving aircraft occur in one particular area? What is the mysterious force causing them?

Countless hours have been spent trying to answer these questions. So far, no one has come up with the final solution to the mystery.

There is another strange factor encountered in these cases of unexplained aircraft accidents that involves a condition of vertigo or disorientation. Under such conditions the pilot is unable to determine the relationship between his aircraft and the ground. He cannot tell whether he is flying up or down, spinning, or in what direction he is headed.

In many of the flight records—tape recordings kept at the various traffic control centers of conversations between pilots and controllers—the evidence indicates that at the time of some of these accidents the pilot was unable to determine his craft's attitude in relation to the horizon, and his instruments failed to be of any use.

What makes these reports more puzzling is that the weather reports for those particular areas show that the conditions at the time were ideal or close to it. Yet the pilots reported that they were flying through some sort of fog or mist that made it impossible to see the ground or the horizon.

Other pilots have encountered an intense heat buildup inside their cabins or cockpits. This sudden condition has caused sufficient concern among some pilots to make them parachute to earth.

If these conditions are due to imagination on the part of pilots or crews, some of whom have thousands of hours of experience, then there must be some mechanism operating in this region that produces false information. Further, it would seem that this mechanism causes pilots to suspend reality and fly their aircraft down glide paths and directly into the concrete runways as if they believed they were still hundreds of feet in the air. In other instances pilots have requested landing instructions from control tower operators, gone through approach procedures, then vanished from control tower radar screens and have never been seen again.

This type of "flyaway accident" is the most frustrating for the accident investigators. All they have is the flight records from the control tower tapes but little else. These records do not indicate that the pilot was experiencing any difficulty.

One pilot who did report that he was having some problem radioed his wingman in an accompanying jet. This case occurred August 2, 1956, while two CF-100 interceptors of the Canadian Armed Forces were flying northwest of Lake Ontario. In his report the flight leader stated that the other pilot had radioed that he was having a problem with vertigo. He then broke formation and vanished. No trace of this jet interceptor or its crew was ever found.

The file on this aircraft, number 18448, was stamped SE-CRET and put away.

A few months before the above incident, on May 5, 1956, another CF-100 interceptor was streaking across the sky northeast of Lake Ontario at thirty thousand feet. The pilot made a routine call to his base and, immediately after making the call, he vanished from the radar screens. Minutes later the base was notified that the jet had plowed into a convent.

How was this possible?

During the transmission, the jet's pilot had been logged at thirty thousand feet and he had said nothing to indicate that he was aware of any problem aboard his aircraft. Yet in an instant he had plunged from thirty thousand feet to zero!

In a communication with the Canadian Defence Headquarters I was informed that the jet was so totally destroyed that it was impossible to determine what had caused this crash.

What happened in so short a span of time? Had he, too, slammed into an invisible wall in the sky, leaving the wreckage to plunge down through a convent roof? Or was this another illogical vertical dive at high speed? In any event, this file is also marked "cause unknown."

No one will ever know if the crew aboard the tug *F. C. Barnes* were suffering from vertigo, disorientation, or invisible walls. Witnesses who saw the tug sailing along the north shore of Lake Ontario stated that as she moved along slowly she entered a cloud of fog or mist that was hanging close to the water. She was never seen again.

This event occurred in the fall of 1915. The shipping season had come to a close and the tug was on her way back to

Kingston for the winter lay-up. Her route took her through the edge of the Marysburgh Vortex but there is no evidence that this caused any concern among the captain or crew.

It was never learned just what this small cloud of fog or mist was. There was no sound of an explosion after the tug disappeared into it. However, when the cloud dissipated a short time later, the tug was nowhere to be seen. When a search was made for debris or an oil slick, there was not a shred of evidence to show that the tug had been in the area. After several days of fruitless searching for the *F. C. Barnes*, the authorities gave up and the disappearance was listed as "unexplained."

Why hadn't the crew of the tug skirted the fog, if only as a safety precaution? No one will ever know.

The slow speed of the *F. C. Barnes* certainly would have allowed the captain to take evasive action to avoid passing through the fog. Not so in the case of the disappearance of Captain George Donner. While sailing up the Great Lakes in 1937 he vanished from the *O. M. McFarland*.

On April 29, the Cleveland *Press* carried a report about the captain's strange disappearance while the ship was still in open water on its way up the lake. And in 1966 Dwight Boyer recounted events aboard the *O. M. McFarland* in his book *Strange Adventures on the Great Lakes*. At 10:15 P.M. on the night of April 28, 1937, Captain Donner gave orders to the second mate to call him when they neared their destination, then went to his cabin.

Several hours later the mate went to the cabin and rapped on the door repeatedly without receiving an answer. Concerned that something might be wrong, he called the first mate but he, too, failed to get a response. When he opened the door Captain Donner was not in his cabin.

A careful search of the ship turned up no clues as to the whereabouts of the captain. Members of the crew reported that he had been seen going into his cabin and heard moving about, presumably finishing up some paperwork; then silence. At no time had he been seen coming out of his cabin.

When the ship reached port another search was made of the vessel, and crew members were questioned individually by authorities. The investigators ruled out suicide and it was suggested that Donner might have fallen overboard while walking on the deck, even though none had seen him leave his cabin. But this was discounted because the weather during the trip had been calm and it was difficult to believe that such an experienced sailor had simply tripped and fallen overboard.

Ships along the *McFarland*'s route were asked to keep a watch for Donner's body, and the same request was passed on to communities along the shore.

Captain Donner's body never did turn up, and his disappearance from his cabin aboard the ship in the middle of the lake is as much a mystery now as it was in 1937.

If there is a mysterious force gathering up people from this region, then that force appears capable of violence in order to have its way. An example of this violence is well demonstrated in the case of the *Eleanor Hamilton* in 1854. What's more important, the crew of this ship seemed to know that something out on the lake was waiting for them.

As the crew prepared the ship for a fall voyage down Lake Ontario, they became reluctant to make the trip. They sensed that certain doom was awaiting them out on the lake and they told the captain of their premonitions. But the captain was a practical man; he put no stock in such feelings. He scoffed at the men's fears and ordered the preparations to continue. When the crew persisted and tried to have the voyage postponed, the captain became boastful. There was no power on the face of the earth that could take his ship from him, he claimed. And the preparations were completed.

When the lines were finally cast off, the *Eleanor Hamilton* sailed out into the Marysburgh Vortex under a moonless sky. That was the last voyage the *Eleanor Hamilton* or her crew ever made. It was also the last time her captain ever made a boast.

None was ever seen again.

Days later the remains of the vessel began to wash ashore along the north side of the lake. Among the splintered wreckage were bits and pieces of decking, cabins, and the hull. Along with this debris came stumps of the sheared-off masts to attest to the violent end this ship had met.

If nothing else, this wreckage was evidence of one thing: Something akin to a giant fist had slammed down on the vessel and turned her into kindling while she sailed through the blackness of the night.

Those who examined the wreckage on the beach knew where the rest of the ship was. But what had become of her crew? Their bodies were not washed ashore in the days and months that followed. No trace of these men was ever found. It was almost as if they had been removed from the ship before it was reduced to firewood.

Had they—like the crew of the *Bavaria*—vanished from the ship *before* it was crushed? And just what was this force that crushed the vessel?

Had modern techniques been available, they might have assisted investigators in uncovering a solution to the puzzling destruction of the *Eleanor Hamilton*. However, even today there are times when such techniques fail to provide the answers.

While the events taking place in this region today appear mysterious and perplexing, one that occurred in the early 1800s would have been classified as astounding. This particular case involved a shipload of government dignitaries and a gigantic stone monolith weighing hundreds of tons. All of these vanished without a trace!

This single most mysterious event took place in Lake Ontario's eastern end in the fall of 1804, when the Canadian government ship *Speedy* vanished along with her crew and passengers.

Present-day records of this event contain the cryptic words "lost on the lake" to explain this disastrous occurrence. But nowhere in these records is there any mention of the mysterious role played by a three-hundred-foot-high, forty-foot-square stone monolith that had been discovered submerged in the lake, and to which this vessel seemed strangely drawn before they both vanished.

In the oft-told versions of the disappearance of the *Speedy*, the story usually begins as the ship prepared to sail from the docks at York (now Toronto) on a Sunday in November 1804. Government officials, representing the majority of the young government of Upper Canada, boarded the ship for the hundred-mile voyage down the lake to Presqu'ile at the eastern end. Among the passengers was an Indian prisoner named Ogetonicut who was being taken to the new town site of Newcastle to be hanged.

After setting sail the *Speedy* made several stops along the lakeshore to pick up other passengers, then the course was set for Presqu'ile Bay. However, the ship was said to have encountered a severe storm and foundered, taking with her all aboard.

That is the simplified version of the saga of the *Speedy* which appears in leaflets and on plaques commemorating this dramatic event. But this version contains nothing about the occurrence that preceded the disappearance of this vessel, or the weird discovery made after the event. These seem to indicate that there were forces at work far more powerful than any government. And they were shaping the history and destiny of this region of North America.

The full story began in the spring of 1804, months before the *Speedy* set out on its fateful voyage. At that time another vessel, the *Lady Murray*, was sailing across the lake toward Presqu'ile Bay on the north side of Lake Ontario. The trip across the lake was uneventful until the ship neared the entrance to the bay. At this point one of the seamen aboard the *Lady Murray* spotted something unusual on the surface of the water. In one small area the waves seemed to be acting strangely in comparison to the water around it.

The seaman brought this anomaly to the attention of the ship's master, Captain Charles Selleck, who also thought it rather peculiar. He ordered the ship stopped and had a boat lowered over the side, and he and some of the crew went to investigate the area at close range.

While the rest of the crew gathered at the rail, Selleck and the others approached cautiously and peered down, seeking the cause of the wave action. At first the answer seemed simple enough. There was a shoal or rock just under the surface. However, a closer examination soon made them change their minds and gave them a healthy respect for that particular area of the lake from then on.

What Selleck and his crew discovered was that this "rock"

was approximately forty feet square and less than three feet under the surface. But when they sounded around it, they learned that the rock's sides dropped straight down for three hundred feet.

This came as a bit of a shock since it was believed that the water at this point was relatively shallow. This so puzzled Captain Selleck that he ordered the soundings done again. The soundings were accurate. The huge stone monolith was sitting upright like a giant tombstone in an incredible fifty fathoms of water!

The find was astounding, to say the least. In fact it was so unusual that when news of it was released, hundreds of local inhabitants came to the site in small boats just to peer down into the depths and sound the area around the strange object themselves.

When Captain Selleck returned to his ship he dutifully recorded the discovery in his logbook. This monolith was a definite hazard to navigation and, although shipping on the lake was still in its infancy, the authorities and other ship's captains would have to be warned.

Over the next few months the site drew many visitors who pushed, probed, and jabbed at the huge stone in an attempt to topple it. But it was immovable and solid.

Among the visitors to this site was Captain Thomas Paxton of the government schooner *Speedy*. It was brought to his attention by Captain Selleck, who personally took him to the site to alert him to the danger that the monolith posed for ships approaching the bay. No one recorded what Paxton's reactions were, yet he was destined by fate to become deeply involved with this submerged mystery before many months had passed.

It was around this same time that the Indian named Ogetonicut was accused of killing a white man at a small settlement just north of the lake. He had been living with members of his tribe, who were camped for the summer on the islands that form Toronto's bay. When caught, he was taken into custody and held for trial.

However, the trial raised some legal problems. The murder had been committed in another district and the law required that the trial be held there. But there were no suitable court facilities available in that district and no proper center for government activities. This sent the ponderous wheels of bureaucracy into motion and a solution was soon arrived at. A temporary courthouse would be arranged at the site at Presqu'ile Bay. Ogetonicut could then be tried and hanged, and the occasion would serve to establish that location as the new town of Newcastle.

With this decided, arrangements were made for the government schooner *Speedy* to transport Judge Thomas Cochrane, court officials, and a selected group of dignitaries who were to officiate over the establishment of the new town.

Strangely enough, the *Speedy* had two alternate captains. One was Paxton and the other was James Richardson. On this trip it was Captain Richardson's turn to act as master of the government ship. But it turned out that Richardson had a deep foreboding about the trip and he tried to persuade the officials to put it off. They in turn rejected the idea of postponing what was planned as a gala event. Richardson persisted in his warnings and was told to step aside and allow Captain Paxton to command the ship. When his warnings of doom failed, he gave the command to Paxton, then tried to alert some of the others who were to board the ship.

In the end Richardson's warnings were ignored and the ship was prepared for departure.

The passengers who boarded the vessel that day were all destined to meet their fate on that voyage, including two young children, who had been put aboard by their parents and left in the captain's charge. There had not been enough money to purchase passage for the whole family. After exchanging good-byes the parents set out to walk the one hundred miles to Presqu'ile. They never saw their children again. The only unwilling passenger on the *Speedy* was Ogetonicut. He had no choice and was taken aboard in chains.

The stops along the lake were to pick up witnesses to the crime. However, some inner sense had warned the witnesses against the voyage and they traveled overland all night to reach Presqu'ile the next day.

Those along the shore who witnessed the storm that night said that it possessed a fury never before seen on the lake. Some claimed that it pursued the vessel up the lake. By midnight, huge waves were battering the shores while the wind made banshee sounds as it tore through the trees.

Under such conditions, and considering the dignitaries aboard, it might have seemed natural for the captain to have sought shelter at some point; however, he steered single-mindedly toward Presqu'ile Bay. At the height of the storm, bonfires were lit along the shore to help guide the ship into safe harbor. Yet the captain paid them no heed. Nor did he appear to have control of his vessel, for her course seemed unerring. As if drawn by a huge magnet, the ship headed directly for the area of the monolith, then was lost from sight as the storm closed over the scene.

When the *Speedy* failed to make port next day, a search was begun along the shore. When the skies cleared, ships took up the search on the lake and passed the word to the

American side that a vessel was missing and searchers there combed the beaches for wreckage.

As days passed without any news of the ship or her passengers, it was decided to drag the area around the monolith in case the ship had collided with the dangerous obstruction and gone to the bottom. But the searchers were in for a surprise. When they reached the location off Presqu'ile Bay they were unable to find any trace of the monolith. When they dragged the bottom they were even more surprised because there were no three-hundred-foot depths in the area. The entire thing had been filled in overnight! The bottom was now shallow and sandy.

The loss of the *Speedy* decimated the government and courts of Upper Canada, wiping out the cream of officialdom overnight. And it had done more. People were now beginning to question many of the strange elements in the whole affair. They wanted to know what the stone monolith had been; if it had been there over the years why had this single storm toppled it? Why had the *Speedy* headed directly for that area when her captain could have grounded her and saved all aboard? Further, what had filled in the three-hundred-foot hole so suddenly?

No one had the answers.

By the law of averages, there should have been a very large pile of stones on the bottom if the *Speedy* had collided with the monolith and toppled it. There was no such pile. If the ship had hit the monolith, then it should have sunk on or near the site and the debris and wreckage should have turned up on the nearby shore. There was no such wreckage that could be linked to this ship.

If neither the monolith nor the ship was in the area, then

the natural question is: What kind of force could transport the entire multiton stone slab and the vessel to regions unknown?

Such a force is beyond what we normally think of as being natural; it is supernatural!

Considering all the various elements that were combined in this single event, it is a strange coincidence that could gather them all in one place. Ogetonicut never died the death of a murderer. Those who sought to impress their ideas on the young government of Upper Canada were removed, and the development of the north side of the lake was set back years by the disaster.

It seems as if the monolith acted like a magnet. When it had gathered all the elements together it eliminated them; then it was no longer needed and it, too, was eliminated.

It will never be known for sure whether the *Speedy* was still under the control of Captain Paxton as she was swept to the site of the monolith, or whether she was under the control of some unknown outside force. If it was the latter, then she isn't the only ship to find herself possessed by masters not of this world. For some, there was the attraction that drew them onto rocky shores; others simply sailed into a fog and vanished; still others were reduced to kindling.

1. & 2. Top, at Prince Edward Point, west of Kingston, the shores of Lake Ontario narrow in, funneling the waters of the Great Lakes through the Marysburgh Vortex and into the St. Lawrence River. Bottom, these deceptively peaceful waters off Prince Edward Point have claimed many ships. This picture is taken looking right into the heart of the vortex. (Hugh Cochrane photos)

3. & 4. CF-100s of the type shown above have vanished in midair or gone into unexplained vertical dives while on routine missions around the Great Lakes. (Canadian Forces photo) U. S. Coast Guard ships and planes are on constant patrols on the lakes. When they arrived at the position given for the missing aircraft N404SA, they searched for wreckage or an oil slick on the water. They found nothing. N404SA was added to the long list of missing planes and vessels. (U. S. Coast Guard photo)

5. Arnold Friberg's painting depicting Joseph Smith receiving the book of gold pages from Moroni, last prophet of an ancient American people. (Reprinted by permission of the Church of Jesus Christ of Latter-Day Saints)

6. This sketch is all that remains of the *Speedy*, which disappeared in the Marysburgh Vortex during a terrible storm in 1804. (John Ross Robertson Collection, Metropolitan Toronto Library Board, JRR1199)

# 3 The Record of Strangeness

Be assured that the forces at work in the Lake Ontario region are not the invention of writers who have researched the history of this eerie domain. Nor are these forces limited to the few hundred square miles of the eastern end of the lake. At times these forces erupt with fury throughout the Great Lakes region, releasing invisible and destructive energies through the waters, the earth, and the skies over this part of the continent.

At times it appears as if some violent force were transmitting its powers along deep subterranean channels or networks in a sort of energy grid capable of routing these disturbances to specific locations. Along the way they are beamed upward, producing nodes and fountains of invisible radiation which propagate fantastic and unexpected effects on matter and the human mind.

Admittedly, a great portion of the losses occurring in this region can be attributed to severe or freak weather conditions. But there still remains a residue of unexplained losses that cannot be simply swept aside.

A glance at old shipping records, newspaper accounts, or old diaries bears out the fact that this region is particularly prone to freak weather conditions and accidents that raise the total losses in vessels and human lives to unusually high figures.

The following is an example from a recent newspaper article reviewing some of these events during a period of approximately twenty years:

| SHIPS | LIVES LOST |
|---|---|
| 1944, April, *James H. Reed*, sank L. Erie | 10 |
| 1944, November, *Ann G. Minch*, sank L. Michigan | 57 |
| 1947, September, *Milverton*, sank St. Lawrence | 15 |
| 1947, June, *Emperor*, sank L. Superior | 12 |
| 1949, September, *Noronic*, burned L. Ontario | 119 |
| 1950, December, *Sachem*, sank L. Erie | 12 |
| 1953, May, *Henry Steinbrunner*, sank L. Superior | 17 |
| 1958, November, *Carl D. Bradley*, sank L. Michigan | 33 |
| 1966, November, *Daniel J. Morrell*, sank L. Huron | 28 |

This list of nine ships and 303 victims is the result of fires, sinkings, or presumed sinkings of vessels that vanished. It in no way equals the previous example shown for 1883; nor does it include the numerous small craft lost on these waters or the numbers of aircraft that were lost by explained, or unexplained, means throughout this region during the same period.

If the invisible forces operating in this area appear to be mysterious, they are no more so than the records being kept of the disasters. Some of the official records seem to overlook some of the major disasters that are recorded elsewhere; others show gaps during years when local newspapers and shipping records show an astounding toll of unexplained losses.

According to the Public Affairs Officer at the Ninth Coast

Guard District at Cleveland, Ohio, no government agency keeps a list of casualties resulting in loss specifically for the Great Lakes. A forty-five-page list of shipping casualties issued by the Canadian Department of Transport is said to cover *all* inland shipping losses across Canada for the years 1870 through 1973—just over one hundred years. The totals on this list show that nine hundred vessels were lost in all Canadian waters, while only two hundred of these occurred on the Great Lakes. Yet a check of old newspapers dating from the 1870s to 1889—approximately twenty years—reveals totals for all events in which vessels have either been sunk, burned, wrecked, grounded, or mysteriously disappeared reaching a staggering six thousand vessels!

Willis Metcalfe, a writer and historian of marine events in the eastern end of Lake Ontario, looked into this matter. He notes that during the years 1910 to 1922 the Donnelly Wrecking Company of Kingston salvaged 283 vessels. He goes on to record that during the week of November 12, 1856, twenty to thirty vessels were lost on Lake Ontario during a storm of unusual severity.

More recent records show that the same pattern was continuing in 1913. In November of that year a four-day period racked up totals of forty vessels and 672 lives!

Among the events that plague this region are cases where there is evidence of a sudden unexplained heat buildup aboard ships or planes that results in a rapidly spreading fire that destroys them.

In September 1949, the passenger steamship *Noronic* was moored at Pier 9 on Toronto's waterfront. This Great Lakes cruise ship had just arrived from Detroit and Cleveland where it had picked up passengers for a cruise to Lake Ontario. The overnight stop at Toronto was to allow passengers time for shopping and sightseeing about the city; some of them remained aboard along with fifteen of the regular crew of 171.

During the evening the stand-by crew prepared the ship for the 7 A.M. departure. But around 1 A.M. a fire burst out in a linen locker on a lower deck and raced through the ship, turning it into a holocaust in minutes. Although the stand-by crew made a heroic effort to put out the fire and get the passengers ashore, 119 fell victim to the blaze.

The actual cause of this fire was never determined.

The *Noronic* was one of three such passenger vessels owned by the Canada Steamship Lines. The other two were the *Harmonic* and the *Quebec*. In July 1945—four years before the *Noronic* burst into flames—the *Harmonic* had been reduced to ashes in a fire said to be of unknown origin.

In August 1950, the stunned officials of the Canada Steamship Lines received the news that the *Quebec*, the last of the trio, had been consumed in a sudden fire while on the St. Lawrence River.

In July 1954, an F-94 jet interceptor of the United States Air Force was scrambled into the skies near the south shore of Lake Ontario. The object causing the alert was a disk-shaped UFO, which had been sighted in the sky to the west of Griffiss Air Force Base. While the base radar operators tracked the UFO on their screens and vectored the jet toward its target, the aircraft streaked across the sky, closing the distance between itself and the strange metallic-like object. Then something happened.

According to the story the pilot gave to a local news reporter shortly after the event, the interior of the jet suddenly became superheated. The pilot alerted his base to the problem, and minutes later he and his radarman were forced to eject from the aircraft when it threatened to burst into flames around them. While they parachuted to earth their plane took a different course. It finally slammed into the town of Walesville, New York, exploding and setting off numerous fires that all but consumed the small town.

After the pilot and radarman had been picked up and transported back to the base, the Air Force released a statement saying that the pilot of the jet had experienced engine failure, which brought about the crash of his jet. The report made no mention of the pilot's original statement to the newsman.

The following brief account reveals a few of the fires of unknown origin which have plagued this area over the years.

Early in November 1873, a rapid series of explosions of unknown cause rocked the vessel *Bavarian* while she was crossing the eastern end of Lake Ontario. Within minutes the ship became a blazing inferno. Those able to escape the flames by jumping overboard were faced with death in the chilling waters and only a few managed to reach a nearby vessel that had come to their aid. At the time it was thought that the captain had been consumed in the flames. However, a month later his body turned up on a beach twenty-five miles away from the scene of the disaster.

In October 1889, another fire of unexplained origin swept the vessel *Quinte* while it was carrying passengers through a bay on the north shore of the lake. Fortunately the captain was able to beach the vessel and allow those aboard to escape, but not before the fire had claimed four lives.

In the spring of 1930, a sudden fire raged through the steam barge *Charles Horn* and its cargo of coal as it sailed through the eastern end of the lake. In short order the vessel burned to the waterline and the remains went to the bottom.

Her four crewmen were able to escape and were rescued by a passing ship.

There are some cases on record that make it appear that it is almost impossible to escape the forces in this region. For some, escape has only been a postponement of their eventual fate. This appears to have been the case in the strange events surrounding the freighter *Star of Suez*.

On June 30, 1964, this ten-thousand-ton freighter sailed into the Marysburgh Vortex and immediately began having trouble. Her navigation equipment began to act erratically and the vessel went miles off course, then ran aground on the north shore at Salmon Point. Tugs were called to her aid and freed the vessel. An investigation of this accident failed to uncover what had caused the navigation equipment to act abnormally. Despite this, the *Star of Suez* continued on her way. The following year the ship returned to the Marysburgh Vortex from the opposite direction. As she neared this zone of mystery a fire suddenly broke out in her hold. When the fire started to get out of control, a distress call was sent out and a nearby vessel came to the aid of the stricken ship and helped to quell the blaze. Without this quick aid the *Star of Suez* would have become another in the long list of statistics. The true cause of this fire was never determined.

A few months after this strange event, and in exactly the same location where the *Star of Suez* had its first encounter with these strange forces, the Greek freighter *Protostatis* ran afoul of the Marysburgh forces (see page 21). As we know, the *Protostatis* did not escape its fate either.

Often mentioned in the reports made by those who have experienced some of these events are feelings of nausea or disorientation. These conditions can make it difficult, if not impossible, for a crew to carry out normal duties.

At the beginning of December 1942, the one-million-gallon tanker barge *Clevco* was being towed through the western end of Lake Erie by the ninety-foot steel tug *Admiral*. Visibility dropped somewhat as the evening approached, but this caused no concern among those in charge since both vessels were equipped with the latest radio communication and navigation devices.

Nonetheless, the crew of the *Clevco* were alarmed when they discovered that the towline connecting them to the powerful tug did not go straight across the water in the normal fashion. Instead, it angled sharply down toward the bottom of the lake. This seemed impossible since, as far as they knew, the *Admiral* had not sunk. There had been no radio calls suggesting any trouble aboard the tug.

The captain of the *Clevco* immediately contacted the tug's owners and the United States Coast Guard and explained the situation. When he gave his exact location, no one expected that the *Clevco* would be going anywhere since it had the *Admiral* on the end of the cable for an anchor.

The facts proved differently.

When the Coast Guard cutters *Ossipee* and *Crocus* arrived on the scene, they found nothing. After circling the area, the officer in charge of the mission put in a call to the Coast Guard base for an aircraft to aid in the search. A short time later an aircraft from the Civil Air Patrol arrived on the scene and widened the search area. When the pilot spotted the *Clevco* it was sixteen miles east of the location given by the captain of the tanker. The aircraft was instructed to hold its position over the *Clevco* until the cutters reached her.

However, while they were on their way it began to snow

heavily. Now the pilot was not only losing track of the tanker, but also the shore. When the ship finally faded from sight, the aircraft was forced to return to its base.

Using the new position given to them by the spotter plane, the cutters zeroed in on the location of the tanker but were unable to make a visual contact because of the snow. In a radio communication with the *Clevco*, they got its new position and headed for that location and were able to make visual contact momentarily when the snow let up. But as they prepared to fire a line to the tanker, it again vanished into the swirling snow and was lost.

At this point the commanding officer aboard the *Ossipee* contacted the *Clevco* and requested the tanker to discharge oil, which would float on the surface and act as a guide for the cutters.

It is not known for certain whether the tanker discharged the oil because it was already too late: the two Coast Guard cutters had now developed problems of their own. A fire had mysteriously broken out aboard the *Crocus*, and by the time her crew got it under control they were forced to return to their base because of the damage.

This left the *Ossipee* to continue the search alone—but not for long. As the lake became rougher the cutter's gyro compass suddenly ceased to function and, surrounded by a curtain of white, they were unable to chart their position or know whether they were going in the right direction. Then the steel vault in the *Ossipee's* main cabin tore loose from its bolts and slammed into the opposite wall!

As if this wasn't enough, members of the crew began to get sick and could no longer carry out their duties. The *Ossipee* never did find any trail of oil on the surface. It was forced to abandon the search and try to find its own way back to its base.

This was the last contact anyone ever had with the *Clevco*. She was never seen or heard from again. Whatever had sucked the steel tug *Admiral* to the bottom of the lake and held it there also claimed the tanker *Clevco*.

This unusual case has been studied by many writers of Great Lakes mysteries, but none has ever been able to find the final solution to the loss of those two vessels.

With the number of unexplained fires that have broken out aboard ships in these waters it might appear safer to stay ashore. Yet the records show that the land around the Great Lakes region has also had a large number of unexplained fires, some of which have lasted for days and racked up losses totaling millions of dollars before they were extinguished.

Take, for instance, the great fire that swept through Chicago on October 8 and 9, 1871. During these two days this city on the edge of Lake Michigan was a raging inferno that consumed three and a half square miles of homes, stores, offices, and factories. Many of the ships in the harbor were reduced to burned-out hulks while the city was turned into rubble. When the fire was finally extinguished an investigation was begun to determine the cause. Investigators turned up the fact that during the two days the fire had lasted, fires had continuously broken out across the city. Investigators did not seem satisfied that all of these were due to flying sparks. They had learned from witnesses that, during the fire, the sky over various portions of the city had taken on an electric-blue and pink glow at times. Also, near the ground similar fluorescent-like glows were reported. Many of the witnesses expressed the belief that something in the air or coming out of the earth caused the fires to erupt, then fed them until the entire city was ablaze.

There is no indication that the cause of the reported glows

was ever discovered. Nor were the investigators in agreement as to what had actually set off the blaze. It is still a mystery.

Like Chicago, Toronto also sits on the edge of one of the Great Lakes. On April 19, 1904, a fire broke out in the midtown section. For hours, firemen fought a losing battle trying to control the blaze. Each time they seemed to be getting the upper hand a strong wind would spring up and fan the flames to a fury, causing them to leap the sixty-six-foot gap across streets and ignite still other blocks of buildings. Neither brick walls nor dynamiting whole buildings effectively stopped the blaze. It was like a demon let loose.

At the height of the fire, calls for assistance went out to fire companies as far away as Buffalo, New York. Yet two days later the fire was still in progress and the whole of the midtown core lay in smoldering ruins. For a further two weeks the fire departments were repeatedly called as blazes broke out again and threatened to start the holocaust all over again.

With five thousand people now unemployed and 104 buildings reduced to ashes, investigators set about the task of sifting through the ruins to find out what had caused the disaster. Among the seemingly improbable causes was one offered by a witness who claimed he had seen some empty wooden crates topple over in an alley and suddenly burst into flames. Finally the fire investigators were forced to admit that they were uncertain of the exact cause of the fire.

It seems that such huge fires are not unusual in this area. Anyone researching the history of this region will come across other fires that have suddenly burst out elsewhere. But what may have been the greatest conflagration of all is one reported to have occurred before the arrival of the white settlers in this area.

G. Copeway, or Kah-Ge-Ga-Gah-Bowh, a chief of the Ojibway nation, recounted the history of the north shore of Lake
Ontario in a book he wrote to explain his people and their
ways. In a chapter describing his youth, he told of his travels
around the north shore and as far west as Lake Huron. The
area he describes is vast—covering approximately ten thousand square miles—yet he describes it in those days as barren,
saying that the forests had been swept away in a great fire
that engulfed the area and consumed everything. In its wake
was left the barren granite hills and rocky crags and peaks.

The exact time of this fire is unknown. Copeway lived from
1818 to 1863, thus it may have occurred during the latter part
of the 1700s. At that time the area must have had a large pop-
ulation of native people, some traders and missionaries. However, they left no accurate accounts of any mass evacuation of
villages. What the toll in human lives was, or how the fire
had begun, will never be known.

In 1968 while gathering material for historical articles on
the early days of settlement around the Great Lakes and the
events involving American and British naval forces, I was astounded at the number of vessels and the manner in which
some of them met their doom in those waters. This was particularly true of the eastern end of Lake Ontario.

A check of historical records covering the operations of
naval forces during the War of 1812 reveals some rather curious facts. One of them is the fact that no major naval engagements ever took place on Lake Ontario. This seems odd because it was here that the greatest naval forces were
assembled by both powers and many of the land offenses
along the shores required long supply lines, which could have
been aided by making full use of these forces.

The commanders and officers on the ships in this region were drawn from experienced naval squadrons, both American and British. By the time the war was drawing to a close the forces on Lake Ontario had at their disposal triple-deck, 120-gun ships manned by close to a thousand men each. They even had available to them Congrave rockets of the type used by the British during the attack on Washington. In short, they had a more powerful force and larger ships than anything Lord Nelson had at the battle of Trafalgar. Yet the records show that the engagements undertaken by these forces on Lake Ontario were little more than hit-and-run encounters in which no decisive action ever took place. In each encounter both sides were eager to break off as quickly as possible and return to the safety of their ports. As the commanders were quick to point out when questioned about this, "Certain conditions on this lake were not favorable to such action."

"Certain conditions?" Or something unnatural?

Included in the plans for the American invasion of Canada during this war was a campaign in which American forces were to strike at Kingston on the north shore, then drive east down the St. Lawrence River to Montreal. Supplies for this attack were taken from American forts at the western end of the lake and transported by ships and small boats along the south shore to be landed at Grenadier Island at the eastern end.

Not one of the fifteen transports used in this movement of munitions and supplies ever reached the marshaling point at Grenadier Island. All vanished during the trip and were never seen again. The ill-equipped American forces went into battle on a modified plan and met disaster at the Battle of Crysler Farm, and the invasion crumbled.

At one point during this war two American vessels—the

110-ton *Scourge* and the 112-ton *Hamilton*—were returning to the fort at Niagara. As they neared their destination both vessels unaccountably turned upside down and sank. With them went ninety of their crews of one hundred. Those who survived were stunned by the event and were unable to explain what had happened to cause both vessels to topple over.

Even John Graves Simcoe, who in 1791 became the first lieutenant governor of Upper Canada (now Ontario), had little use for these waters. From the first time he sailed on Lake Ontario, he expressed a dislike for these waters which ". . . could change with strange suddenness."

Simcoe was well acquainted with the wide oceans of the world. He had served the British Government in many other colonies and had traveled thousands of miles over open sea. So why did he look with disfavor on this particular stretch of water?

Part of the answer may be revealed in the meticulously kept diary of the lieutenant governor's wife. One of her entries states that on their arrival in the area, the St. Lawrence River and parts of Lake Ontario were rocked by an earthquake. Some of the shocks came as often as thirty times a day and alarmed the new inhabitants.

In another entry she reveals that after the earthquakes a strange sight was seen in the sky. Mysterious "globes of light" appeared from the southwest—from eastern Lake Ontario— and moved across the sky to the northeast following the St. Lawrence River.

These "globes of light" were observed on several occasions by numerous witnesses and were also recorded in the early newspapers of that day. Some of the observers stated their belief that the phenomenon might be coming from a volcano. This is unlikely since no volcanoes have existed in this area of the continent in recent times. However, there were volcanoes in the St. Lawrence and Ontario regions during a very early geologic period, most traces of which were swept aside during glacial periods thousands of years ago.

One of the most curious accounts to appear in Mrs. Simcoe's diary is one for December 31, 1791. She records this date as the anniversary of an event which a few years before had brought a great blackness that covered the sky. So dark was it that candles had to be lit in the middle of the day, and people walking on the other side of the street could not be seen.

Other accounts of this event make it clear that the strange blackness rolled in from the eastern end of Lake Ontario at a low level and it was claimed that this was not smoke or clouds. No one at the time was able to determine just what was the composition of this black mass.

Add strange globes of light and darkness in the sky to the frost fogs, areas of reduced binding, odd attractions, vanishing ships, and a strange monolith. No other area on earth has produced such a fantastic array of enigmas. Not even the famed Bermuda Triangle!

When it comes to things disappearing in this area, size does not seem to matter. Islands, for example, appear to have vanished. Very large ones.

When the French explorer Samuel de Champlain arrived on this continent in 1632, he set about mapping and exploring many of its features. It was his intention to provide a fairly accurate set of maps of the New World while he sought a route to China. He began the task on the Atlantic coast and worked his way through bays, coves, and inlets, then finally up through the St. Lawrence Valley, following the great river

to the southwest. Along the way he noted islands and major
rivers plus numerous adjoining lakes. All of these were included on his working maps, most of which are now preserved
in museums in France.

Because Champlain's time was limited, he couldn't explore
every river and stream or follow them to their source. Often
he had to rely on others, such as his aide Étienne Brulé or the
Indians who were serving as guides. They either scouted the
areas for him or were able to supply information from
firsthand knowledge of the uncharted areas.

Champlain's maps had a good percentage of accuracy, as
can be seen in the distances between locations or the positions of various features. But there is one map that is out-
standing for its inaccuracy. It was made during an expedition
that took Champlain up the St. Lawrence and Ottawa rivers,
then north to the portages that eventually led to the Georgian Bay. From here he worked his way through rivers and
lakes until he came out on the shores of Lake Ontario near
the entrance to the St. Lawrence.

At this point the explorer's supplies were running low and
the season was getting late. He had planned to leave the area
before the freeze-up and this caused him to cut short his explorations. However, since he had found the Indian guides
well informed about other areas, he depended on them to
complete his mapping of Lake Ontario. Thus he was able to
pinpoint major rivers, including Niagara Falls, along with
bays such as Burlington, Sodus, and Quinte. There was even a
good representation of the long moccasin-like shape that is
characteristic of Lake Ontario.

Although the map was, for the most part, accurate, it also
contained glaring oddities. Drawn in were numerous islands,
two of which were very large. One of them was shown located

close to Niagara near the American shore, the other on the Canadian side close to Cobourg. The one closest to Canada was drawn on a scale that would have made it close to fifteen miles long and seven miles wide. In fact, either island was shown large enough to accommodate a city the size of today's metropolitan Toronto!

There are no such large islands on this lake today.

Is their presence on Champlain's map due to inaccurate information he was given? If so, why didn't similar mistakes occur on his other maps, which were also prepared with help from these same sources? Or did the two islands actually exist at that time?

It is difficult to imagine that early native inhabitants would conjure up islands where none existed. In this particular area there are over sixty miles of empty horizon, with not even a single rock projecting from the water.

The islands on the map appeared to be within five miles of shore. Therefore they would be impossible to miss and even more impossible to misplace in relation to the rest of the lake. Yet when Louis Jolliet, another explorer, traveled through the area in 1674 or 1679, he did not see them. This raises the question of whether or not they disappeared during the forty years between Champlain's and Jolliet's visits.

Vanishing islands are not a new phenomenon. It has happened many times. Some islands have vanished and then reappeared years later when some geological event raised them to the surface again. However, there is no account of such an event even in the Indian lore of this region.

Some evidence that might support the idea that there were such islands on Lake Ontario at some point in history is indicated by features found on present-day hydrographic maps. These show shallow areas of water just off Alcott, New York, on the American shore and between Colborne and Cobourg on the Canadian shore. The locations of both of these areas are the same as those marked as large islands on Champlain's map.

An underwater investigation of these sites might prove interesting because among the Indian legends are tales of "cities of light" said to be part of a civilization that once inhabited this region. Although evidence of such a group is scant, they, like the legendary Atlanteans, may have lived on a large island which sank beneath the water.

At some time during the early part of the 1500s there appears to have been another little-known case of disappearance that remains unmatched. This, too, occurred close to the eastern end of Lake Ontario.

In 1535, when the explorer Jacques Cartier led an expedition up the St. Lawrence River, he visited native people who were living at Hochalaga (now Montreal) and others living on islands farther up the river near Lake Ontario. In his reports, Cartier said these people were a different group or tribe from those he had met farther down the St. Lawrence. This group had an unusual method of building their villages on various levels in pyramid fashion. This consisted of three mounds of earth, one atop the other, and the whole thing surrounded by a circular wooden enclosure. On the uppermost level up to fifty dwellings were constructed. Cartier offered no explanation of why they used this method of construction. Yet it sounds similar to the constructions built by the Mayans and Incas in Central America.

If these people had connections with the early southern groups, then that evidence is yet to be found. For the present, all that is known for sure is that this tribe vanished. Some seventy years after Cartier's visit, Champlain arrived on the scene, expecting to visit them but he found no such tribe. Each location had been abandoned and there was no trace of the estimated two thousand to four thousand people who had inhabited the area at the time of Cartier's visit.

Present-day anthropologists have tried to trace this vanished tribe without success. It was thought they might have been conquered and absorbed into other tribes; but so far, no evidence has been found to support this theory.

This brings us back to the question we have asked before: Where did they go? Is there one separate place where all these people, ships, planes, islands, and monoliths go?

The records left by these early explorers appears to have provided numerous mysteries that still have not been properly answered. Another curious one is contained in Cartier's records of a meeting he had with tribal chiefs at a point near Lake Ontario when he was preparing for his departure from North America.

A feast had been arranged and during the festivities the chiefs presented the explorer with twelve quill-like rods of gold to take back to his king. When Cartier asked where the golden rods had come from, the chiefs pointed toward southern Ontario and the lake, saying that the rods had come from the "city of Saganna," which was located somewhere to the west. They then went on to astound the explorer by stating that the "city of Saganna" was a place where men flew in the sky like birds!

Early European explorers discounted native claims or records as nothing more than the imaginings of savages. Their legends were considered to be amusing stories told to children by the elderly. This sort of bias closed the minds of these

explorers to many truths, which are only now being redis-
covered. Thus nothing more was learned of this strange city
where men were said to fly like birds. What purpose the
twelve gold rods served will never be known. They were taken
to France by Cartier and in all likelihood were turned into
some bauble to amuse the king.

There are a number of Indian legends that tell of great
shining cities of light that were located close to the Great
Lakes. According to these stories, the inhabitants of these
marvelous cities lived in great homes amid beautiful surroundings. It was from here that men were said to fly into the
skies to meet the thunderbirds when they came down from
the stars bringing ancient gods or great leaders. These legends
also say that certain people were chosen from the tribes to ac-
company these space travelers back to the stars. Other stories
tell of the dark times on earth when the serpents returned to
spread havoc over the land. It was during this time that the
great cities of light were destroyed, leaving nothing but ruin
in their place.

Do these legends come from the colorful imagination of a
group of primitive people? Or are they the fragments of the
history of an actual civilization that existed in ancient times?

There are many locations around the Great Lakes where
the early native Americans recorded in paintings and carvings
the events of historic or local importance. Animals, humans,
and deities are shown participating in various activities. According to the experts who have studied them, the drawings
must be interpreted as elements depicting a whole event
rather than words carrying specific meanings.

Among the locations where these forest archives have been
found is a site on Mazinaw Lake, a short distance north of
the eastern end of Lake Ontario, and in the same general lo-

cation indicated as being the home of the birdmen of the city of Saganna.

Rising straight out of the lake is a massive upthrust of granite with a sheer wall that provides a mile-long surface facing west. On this face the early people painted the symbols and shapes of a sacred or historical nature. This wall contains what has been regarded as the largest collection of early Indian paintings ever found in one place. Their age is still to be determined, but some experts cautiously suggest they may have been painted almost a thousand years ago.

No exact interpretation has been put on these paintings. Nor have experts been able to prove conclusively what group of native people actually did the work. However, one rather interesting painting depicts what has been described as the "rabbit-man" because of what appears to be two very large, flat-topped ears. By the same token, this painting could also be depicting a man with wings. Just the sort of symbol that could be applied to the legendary men of Saganna who could fly in the sky.

Mazinaw Lake is an ideal location for this ancient Indian artwork. The scene presented today by the curtain of granite rising out of the water is at times strange and overpowering, as it must have been in the early days when native people came to record the things important to their culture.

Within sight of this granite mass is a smaller lake named Mississagagon. It, too, has a story that is becoming a legend. For this is a lake mentioned in a tale of treasure told by the early white settlers in this area.

According to this story, at some point around this small lake is a cavern containing a fabulous hoard of silver. To the Indians who lived in this area, the lake was sacred and its location was known only to the shaman, or priest, of the tribe.

But a white trader named Captain Meyer, who lived on the shores of Lake Ontario, learned of the cavern and its treasure from his Indian guide, François. Together they captured the shaman and forced him to take them to the sacred cavern. There they gathered a fortune from the silver that hung from the cavern ceiling like icicles.

But Meyer and François never lived to enjoy their wealth. As they traveled back across the lake the Indians were waiting for them. They attacked them and killed François and the priest for divulging the secret location of the cave, and wounded Meyer. Meyer escaped only to die later from his wounds. But not before he had told his story of the fabulous cave and its treasure.

Many have searched for this cave but none have found it. Like the city of Saganna and the cities of light, its location remains a mystery.

# 4 Visible and Invisible Enigmas

At the beginning of the research into the unexplained events occurring in the Great Lakes region, I found that the phenomena paralleled a pattern that is evident in other zones of mystery around the world. However, the deeper one probes into old records or newspaper accounts, the more convincing the evidence becomes that the mysteries taking place here go far beyond the range of ship disappearances and vanishing crews. Instead, the events run the gamut of forces that affect vessels and aircraft mysteriously, involve human psychic abilities, and bring about encounters with strange beings not of this world. They are also linked with apparitions, lights that come and go without explanation, and even recurring events that emerge from the past.

In all of these there appears to be a fundamental force or power that may prove to be the cause of all the events. Yet this force seems to operate in a variety of ways that results in an element of strangeness in each event. This strangeness appears to be the only consistent element. This fact becomes obvious when cases in this and other chapters are examined closely. In most of these the main event, though inexplicable in itself, is made more so by other elements that seem to have been introduced simply to make the whole event even stranger still.

It was a strange sight that confronted residents of Morristown, New York, and Brockville, Ontario, on February 14, 1915. Aircraft were still relatively new and were an oddity that attracted the public's attention. But for the residents of these two St. Lawrence River communities the aircraft that appeared in the skies above them were more than just an attraction; they were downright weird!

When these three aircraft first passed over during the evening, they caused a commotion because few such machines had ever been seen in that area. When they returned a few hours later, they created an even greater commotion.

According to the accounts that appeared in local newspapers, and in newspapers as far away as New York, these aircraft passed over the river, then returned later, hovering at various places over the communities and shining bright searchlights down on the inhabitants.

According to the account carried in the New York *Times* on February 15, the aircraft were first seen near Gananoque, Ontario, forty miles southwest of the Morristown-Brockville area. At that time the three aircraft were on a northeast course almost paralleling the St. Lawrence River. On the return trip they traveled southwest, pausing along the way.

Just how these objects were able to hover in flight when such aircraft had not been invented is a question difficult to answer. Even more difficult to explain is how such aircraft could carry the equipment necessary to power the powerful searchlights, whose beams, according to witnesses, were swept back and forth, illuminating the communities.

This problem caused enough concern among the residents of Brockville that the mayor requested the Canadian Government to provide an immediate answer. The government's reply suggested that what the residents had seen were balloons, not aircraft. They did not say who the owners of the balloons might be, nor did they attempt to explain how a balloon could hover in a wind or travel in a direction opposite to it!

There is no evidence to indicate that action had been taken by the authorities to identify these "balloons" or their owners, and the sightings continued. By the end of the week other communities along the St. Lawrence River were reporting similar encounters, showing that the phenomenon had been observed along a line stretching fifty miles from Gananoque to Ogdensburg.

It is worth noting that these events occurred in the evening hours and no complete description was supplied other than the impression of observers that the objects were aircraft. In most of the accounts there is the mention that there were three dark objects, and at times each had been accompanied by bright lights. These match the description being supplied today by observers in the same area who are reported to have seen UFOs. In all of these accounts the main feature is a bright light or lights, which also seem to be observed in threes.

If the residents of the St. Lawrence and the eastern end of Lake Ontario thought they were being ignored by the government, they were actually only getting the same treatment that other communities had received two years earlier.

Observers in these communities reported a phenomenon,

in February 1913, that occurred in the western end of Lake Ontario on the Canadian shore. This one was witnessed by numerous people in Toronto who described the late-night sighting as being like a procession of lights that crossed the sky from the northwest to southeast. The total time taken for this phenomenon to pass over Toronto was said to have been five minutes.

Among the witnesses to this event were two astronomers, and these reliable witnesses reported their observations in the Royal Canadian Astronomical Society's journal. One of these astronomers described the sight as being like an express train lighted at night.

The following day a Toronto newspaper, the *Daily Star*, carried an article describing the second sighting. This time the objects were viewed against a bright sky and they appeared dark. Some witnesses thought the objects were airships traveling in groups of three and seven. Again, the course followed by these unidentified objects was from northwest to southeast.

A few days after the event, public curiosity about the strange objects began to fade. Astronomers decided that the evidence indicated that the objects were meteors and this appeared to solve the problem of the strange globes of light in the sky. At least for the time being.

However, the strange globes did not go away. In fact they are still with us today and are being reported by some observers who claim to have seen them a few feet above the ground. This suggests that, while the astronomers may be correct in some cases, there are others which show evidence of something far different from meteors. This something different may include those globes of light reported by Mrs. Simcoe in the late 1700s which may turn out to be part of the

UFO phenomenon so widely reported today. The quantity of these contemporary reports has now reached significantly large proportions, a fact that should attract considerable attention from the scientific community. Instead, most of the reports are simply ignored.

There are more than just globes of light being seen in the sky over the Great Lakes region. Experienced seamen have told of observing weird ghost fleets made up of dozens of vessels seen sailing across the sky as if driven by etheric winds. Others tell of witnessing the passage of early sailing ships that no longer existed at the time of the sighting. All seemed to be floating above the water until they vanished back into their own time.

Experts explain that such sightings are mirages created by the layering of warm and cold air in a manner that causes a lenslike effect which can magnify images and transmit them to a distant observer, who sees what appears to be a real object suspended in the air. In many cases this may be true. But this explanation does not account for the appearance of images of objects that no longer exist at the time they are being seen.

Stranger than these out-of-date sailing ships are the translucent cubes and oblong shapes seen by seamen on these lakes in the 1890s. One seen by several members of a ship was described as an oblong object like a glass case that contained, of all things, a steamship! The whole effect gave the impression that a huge steamship was being transported across the sky inside a glass case of enormous proportions.

According to the definition of a mirage, this may have been the image of a model ship in a glass case housed in some marine museum, the image being magnified and transmitted across hundreds of miles to the observers. However, this explanation is no more difficult to accept than present-day suggestions that the steamship had been "captured" and was being transported from earth by some extraterrestrial beings seeking specimens.

As the skipper of a Lake Ontario pleasure craft once told me, "They may be mirages to a scientist in a lab. But people out on the lake know differently!"

The most notable "mirage" ever seen on Lake Ontario was one that came equipped with its own sound effects. This one appeared in 1910 to the crew of a ship spending the night in Etobicoke harbor. Around 1:30 A.M. members of the crew were awakened by a ship's whistle giving a distress call. When the crew scrambled on deck and looked out toward the lake they saw a steamship, her cabin windows lit with oil lamps and her superstructure visible under a full moon as she moved across the water. Repeatedly, her whistle gave out the four long blasts to indicate that she was in distress.

Some of the crew decided to find out what the trouble was; they lowered a small boat and quickly rowed out into the lake to offer whatever assistance they could. All the while, the screaming whistle urged them on.

However, before they could reach the stricken vessel it vanished before their eyes!

The astounded crewmen sat stunned as they scanned the area in disbelief. Around them, waves, like those that follow the passage of a ship, began rocking their boat. But where was the ship?

Among the eleven witnesses to this extraordinary event was Rowley W. Murphy, a noted Great Lakes historian. His account of the event was published by the Great Lakes Historical Society. In this he stated that the steamship had sounded her whistle in a signal of distress for almost ten minutes, and that the vessel had resembled the early passenger steamships, none of which were in service any longer at the time of the sighting.

Had these crewmen actually seen and heard a mirage? Or had an object from out of the past slipped out of its time frame long enough to cross that threshold we call the present and then moved back into its own time again? If so, then these crewmen almost made contact with another dimension —one that exists just outside our own time.

If it is possible for one material object to pass through the barrier in this way, this might provide a solution to the mystery of what became of the *Picton* ten years before at the opposite end of the lake (see page 13). It might also explain how the captain of the *Picton* found time to write his strange note and seal it into a bottle after he and his vessel had vanished.

While some put their faith in images transported in layers of air, one Buffalo man rejects the whole idea completely.

One afternoon in the summer of 1972, this man (who has requested that his name not be used) decided to do some fishing. He took his boat out into the eastern end of Lake Erie, close to Buffalo, and started to fish. This day, however, the fish were not cooperating and the only thing disturbing the otherwise calm surface was the plop of his lure. But the lake did not remain placid for long. Without warning, what appeared to be a large silver disklike object burst from under the water and shot straight up into the summer sky with such a force that the wave it created almost swamped the fisherman's boat!

Later, this man said that the silver craft was about thirty to forty feet across and had come out of the water less than a hundred yards from his boat. The event had been so sudden and stunning that he could only sit gaping as the craft disappeared high in the sky.

As a result of this close encounter the man no longer fishes in Lake Erie. The thought of what might have happened if the strange craft had been closer to his boat still leaves him in a cold sweat.

There is an interesting follow-up to this case that once again points up the element of strangeness present in this region. In this particular case the fisherman was reluctant to have his name revealed for fear of ridicule. However, he did reveal to an investigator from MUFON (Mutual UFO Network)—a privately funded UFO investigation group—that his was not the only UFO encounter to occur in his family. His wife also underwent a very upsetting experience when she became involved with one of these strange flying objects a week or so later.

Her experience began when she and her daughter saw what appeared to be a glowing ball coming down out of the sky and landing near their home. Becoming curious, they went to investigate or at least to get a closer look at whatever it was. They never did get a close look because as they approached the area the object shot into the air and vanished in the distance.

This experience merely left the woman puzzled, but what happened to her a few days later scared her.

On her way home from work a few days after the incident, the woman discovered that she was being followed by two men in a car. She tried unsuccessfully to dodge them, then went straight home. When she looked out the front window a short time later, she was surprised to see the same two men sitting in their car just down the street. Thinking she might be imagining things, she put the matter aside. But later when she looked out the window again, they were still there. Deciding to take no chances, she called the police. Just a minute or so before the police car rounded the corner, the car started up and the two men quickly drove away.

The woman then decided that she had probably over-reacted and that the whole thing was nothing more than coincidence. But she soon changed her mind again several days later when she discovered she was being followed by the same two men. Without trying to avoid them this time, she drove straight home. When she went to the window she saw that they had again parked down the street. Wasting no time, she called the police and a car was immediately dispatched to the area. Again, just before the police arrived, the car left. This time the police scoured the district but found no trace of the car she had described.

Neither the police nor the UFO investigator ever learned whether the two men in the car were simply there by coincidence or whether there was some purpose for their visit. There was nothing tangible to link them to the strange glowing ball that had landed near the woman's home. Only an inner sense told this woman that it was all part of the same thing.

The UFO investigator who supplied the information on the above case also told me of a similar encounter with a UFO that had occurred a few years before. It had happened to him and had caused him to become seriously interested in UFOs.

In his case he, too, was fishing on Lake Erie close to Buffalo. It was an August afternoon in 1955 and the sun was at his back while he faced east toward shore. Suddenly he was startled by a brilliant light that rose up from behind a factory on the shore and began to approach his boat. As the glow drew closer he said he could make out what appeared to be a bell-shaped object inside the glow. The object seemed to be giving off a bright radiation.

The fisherman made these observations as he sat, puzzled, while the thing rushed toward him. Just as it occurred to him that it was on a collision course with his boat, the object, which had been a few feet above the water, made a sharp right-angle turn before it hit the boat, then disappeared into the distance.

Since this first encounter, this Buffalo man has also had five other experiences with these so-called UFOs but none as close as this breathtaking experience. Several years after the event, he became aware of the fact that his was not an isolated incident; others had similar experiences at different locations in the Lake Ontario and Lake Erie regions. Having overcome his initial fear brought on by this near-miss, he began documenting evidence from others with similar experiences.

Since this fishing-boat incident, he was pleased to admit, his next encounters were at longer range. In these sightings he described the objects as glowing lights that hovered, changed color from white to orange, then sped off across the night sky faster than a jet aircraft.

While the presence of these unexplained objects speeding back and forth creates a mystery, other objects vanish from the sky and their absence creates a mystery.

On November 3, 1977, Calvin Gavine, an experienced forty-seven-year-old pilot, and Erik Lind, a thirty-three-year-old engineer, took off from an airport at Marathon, Ontario, on the north shore of Lake Superior, for a flight to Maple on the outskirts of Toronto. Somewhere along this 350-mile-long route the plane with the two men vanished. Although a search was made that lasted several weeks, not a trace of this missing aircraft or its occupants could be found.

During the search, a total of eleven aircraft were used to cover the route and to concentrate on a stretch of bushland along the north shore of Lake Superior. The bush here is a dense maze of rock, swamp, and jackpine that claims an average of a hundred lives a year. Most are hunters and fishermen, 20 percent of whom drown. Many of those who become lost in this area and survive are found staggering about half mad.

Mac Nicholson, who leads a private search and rescue group of two hundred seventy-five volunteers equipped with trucks, snowmobiles, aircraft, and boats, has taken searchers into this 45,000-square-mile area numerous times and knows how the tangled vastness of the area can crumble the human mind in seconds. "It causes a type of claustrophobia," he told a reporter for the Toronto *Sun*. "Everything just closes in. Their minds go blank and they run themselves to exhaustion. They'll bull blindly through the thickest bush." Nicholson added: "The worst one I've seen, we had to put him into a straitjacket. He ran into the search line and we had to throw him down and hang on to him."

Since 1952 thirty-four people and seventeen aircraft have been swallowed up in this area. All are believed to have plunged into this wilderness. Like Gavine and Lind, no traces of their aircraft were found and their files were closed and stamped "cause unknown."

Then there is the case of Tom Walker (see page 10),

whose route on November 8 was practically the same as the missing November 3 flight, only he was going in the opposite direction.

On December 22, 1977, Craig Carlisle, an American pilot, took off from the airport at Oshawa, on the north side of Lake Ontario, in a twin-engine Cessna, N404SA. His destination was Beaver Falls, Pennsylvania, by way of Buffalo, New York, and the first leg of the flight was over the western end of Lake Ontario.

According to Major Al Ditter, spokesman for the Canadian Forces Base at Toronto, the aircraft left Oshawa at 9 P.M. and in less than half an hour was at midpoint in its flight over the lake. At this point the controllers at Toronto's International Airport handed control of this flight over to the Buffalo controllers.

However, there was a problem. The Buffalo controllers could not find any such flight on their radar screens and they informed Toronto Control of this fact. When the Toronto controllers checked their screens they discovered that they, too, had lost the aircraft's blip. In the minute or so it had taken to transfer the flight, the plane had suddenly vanished.

Carlisle had six thousand hours of flying experience. If he was having some problems with his aircraft, why did he not report it to the controllers when they informed him he was moving into the Buffalo control area? Why had there been no signal from his emergency transmitter, which was designed to send out a signal in the event of a crash?

When notified that this aircraft was missing, the United States Coast Guard, along with a helicopter and a Hercules aircraft from the Canadian Forces Search and Rescue, combed the western end of the lake. After two days of searching this thirty-by-forty-mile stretch of water without any success, the search was called off. No oil slick or debris was found which would indicate that an aircraft had crashed.

Aircraft number N404SA has been added to the long list of others that have mysteriously vanished without a trace. And it had vanished in the most densely populated area bordering Lake Ontario, yet no one had witnessed the event.

On the same day, something even more unusual happened at the other end of the lake. A TWA crew flying at ten thousand feet reported that they had seen a brilliant blue-green light in the sky above their aircraft, and an instant later they spotted a brilliant orange object at a lower altitude near the earth below them. This double flash occurred several times, and each time it occurred all the lights on the ground, in a three- to four-mile area around the orange object, appeared to go out.

Strangely, while all this was going on, newspaper offices and police departments were receiving calls reporting sonic booms that rattled windows over a wide area of New York state.

All of this evidence suggests that there is some sort of connection between these events. At times it seems that behind the mysterious occurrences there is a pent-up violence, which is triggered by forces unknown to science. But while these forces are capable of outbursts of destruction, they are also capable of striking with silent swiftness.

There are waves generated on the Great Lakes that are said to be spawned by powerful forces of seismic or atmospheric origin. These are called seiche waves, and they possess the power of a gigantic battering ram, yet they give no warning of their presence. They seem to come from nowhere, abruptly sweeping into harbors, lifting docks and ships, sweeping away buildings and unsuspecting humans. When their force is spent, they recede back into the lake and vanish as if they had never existed.

In 1954, this type of wave rolled in from Lake Michigan at Chicago, swamping vessels and sweeping fifty fishermen off a pier and into the lake. In this case the weather had not been unusual, there had been no storm in progress, and those swept off the dock had not had the slightest warning of what was about to occur until it was too late.

It was believed that this same sort of seiche wave caused the loss of the tug *Sachem* in Lake Erie in December 1950. The weather was calm when she sailed from Buffalo on her way down the lake to Dunkirk. But she never arrived at her destination, and a search failed to find any trace of her. Then, in January 1951, the bodies of her crew began to wash up on the shore.

By October 1951, the Coast Guard located the *Sachem* sitting on the bottom of the lake and the sunken vessel was raised to the surface and taken into harbor for investigation. An examination revealed that the tug's machinery and hull had been in perfect condition when the tug sank. What puzzled the investigators was that the engine controls in both the pilot house and engine room were in the stop position, and all of the windows in the pilothouse were smashed out. These clues led investigators to believe that the tug had been struck by a huge wave that had filled the vessel with water and sent her to the bottom.

Curiously, when the Coast Guard found this vessel it was

less than two miles from shore, and there had been no reports of any such wave reaching the shore in the surrounding area.

Great Lakes lighthouse keepers are well acquainted with seiche waves, which can vanish just as quickly as they appear. Some experts claim that they can appear hours before a storm on the lake; others suggest that they are spawned deep under the surface of the lake, possibly by seismic events occurring on the lake bottom.

An unusual phenomenon that has been observed many times on Lake Ontario is a slowly rising swell in which waves rise from an otherwise calm surface and gradually rise higher and higher along the shore. After a short period the water slowly recedes, then the whole process begins again. These strange, short-lived tides have been known to continue for from four to eight hours before the lake again returns to normal level.

Such phenomena contribute to the strangeness of the events occurring in this region. But there are more.

# 5 Psychics and Energies

While there is a strong similarity between the unexplained events taking place in the Great Lakes region and those plaguing the Bermuda Triangle, a difference in climate restricts the investigations in the former. The Great Lakes region is locked in the grip of winter storms for three months of the year; the Bermuda Triangle is in a much more temperate zone, giving investigators more time to probe the unexplained events occurring there. As a result, a variety of possible solutions to the mysteries have emerged, ranging from the elegant to the bizarre. The most intriguing of these is the theory proposed by some investigators and writers attributing these events to the outpouring of energy from the huge crystal generator believed to have been constructed by the ancient civilization of Atlanteans (see page 16).

Much of the evidence to support this proposed solution stems from information contained in the psychic readings of Edgar Cayce, America's "sleeping prophet." Although the legend of Atlantis supposedly began with Socrates, writers like Ignatius Donnelly assembled a mass of material from geological, archaeological, and legendary sources to show that such an ancient society did exist. Cayce, on the other hand, supplied his information from psychic sources and produced a convincing portrait of the people and events in that ancient land.

Cayce, like others, placed the location of Atlantis in the Atlantic between Gibraltar and the Caribbean. But his information places it closer to the North American shores.

He received his information while in a trance state, and the Atlantis material was given in connection with other information regarding the past lives of people who sought his aid. His source seems to have been some universal memory bank of records of the past which he called the Akashic records. This may be something similar to what C. G. Jung called the collective unconscious.

What makes Cayce's revelations so astounding was his record for accurately predicting major and minor events that were to take place in the coming years. He was able to predict the beginning and the end of the second great war, and even the discovery of the Dead Sea Scrolls a quarter of a century before the event and before anyone even guessed that such a find might be possible. He attributed these scrolls to the Essenes and revealed much about the information the scrolls contained.

In one of his readings Cayce gave what may be the most important information regarding Atlantis when he stated that the remains of this lost civilization would be discovered in 1969 off Bimini Island in the Bahamas. In 1969 such a discovery seems to have been made. A pilot flying over this part of the Atlantic spotted what appeared to be walls and the remains of buildings under the water. Subsequent investi-

gations have revealed that there are some sort of stone constructions in this underwater region, some of which extend
for miles.

When writers and investigators of Bermuda Triangle mysteries came on this revelation, they were quick to see the possible connection with the problems plaguing this area. Since
then the belief in the Atlantean connection has grown.

A new element was added to the Bermuda Triangle mystery, late in 1977, when another underwater investigator accidentally discovered what appeared to be a submerged pyramid sitting in 1,200 feet of water off the south end of Bimini
Island. The discovery was made when a sonar scanner—depth
finder—aboard a cruiser traced out the outline of a massive
structure, showing it to be 780 feet high and 1,000 feet long
on each side of its base. The whole structure appears to be
sitting on a relatively flat area of the ocean floor.

Whether this pyramid is related to the strange events of
the triangle, or whether it is further proof of the existence of
the ancient civilization of Atlantis as revealed by Edgar
Cayce, is something that still has to be proved. In the meantime, the discovery has added new fuel to the Bermuda mystery and renews the belief in its links with the ancient past.

In September 1977, newspapers carried stories about an international research project to be carried out by Britain, the
United States, Soviet Russia, Canada, and France. The project's main undertaking was an oceanographic survey of the
underwater currents along the western edge of the Atlantic
Ocean, a good portion of which lies inside the Bermuda Triangle.

By November one of the Russian scientists involved in the
project, Vladimir Azhazha, an oceanographer, told news re-

porters some of his theories of a possible connection between the Bermuda Triangle mystery and unusual infrasonic waves being generated in that part of the ocean.

In an interview he explained that the infrasound is generated by distant storms, but is of such a frequency that it is inaudible to the human ear. He further stated that this silent sound may be somehow magnified by special conditions existing in the Bermuda Triangle area.

Other scientists admitted that such a vibration, if it were powerful enough, could be sufficient to bring about the destruction of aircraft or oceangoing vessels. It could cause weak joints in hulls or frames to rupture, even cause the breakdown of the vital machinery.

More important are other discoveries made concerning this silent sound. In Britain and France, for example, experiments have been conducted to determine the effects of infrasound on animals and humans. It was found that weak levels of infrasound can induce seasickness, while higher levels can induce stomach and brain problems. In some cases it was discovered that certain levels could cause blindness.

Such waves can travel great distances underwater, and the Soviet scientists said the Gulf Stream could increase or decrease its effectiveness. Thus, distant storms could be the major factor in the unexplained disappearances of ships, planes, and crews in the Bermuda Triangle simply by the infrasonic sounds they propagate.

Some of the Russian scientists are calling this phenomenon the "Voice of the Sea," and relate the unheard sound waves—at frequencies lower than sixteen cycles per second—to the speed of the wind generated by the storms. Such low frequencies, they point out, could silently reach out across the water, or through it, and bring about the end of a vessel while it sailed in calm waters.

At the beginning of 1977, other researchers were taking a different approach in an attempt to get to the bottom of the Bermuda Triangle mystery. Two noted Dutch psychics were used to probe events to see what they could uncover.

In an article for *Fate* magazine (August 1977), Walter H. Uphoff reported on this work, which was carried out on January 10 and 20, 1977, by the noted Dutch psychics Gerard Croiset and Warner Tholen, and in cooperation with the Dutch Society for Psychical Research.

These two psychics have an impressive record of successes with this type of psychic information-gathering—Croiset has successfully located over eight hundred missing persons using clairvoyant methods of uncovering information. Working on oceanographic maps and photographs, they were able to dowse the Bermuda Triangle and locate centers where forces were erupting from the bottom of the ocean.

Basically, their findings indicate that within the triangle there are natural centers of erupting forces, which they believe are triggered by the passage of the moon's fields—gravitational and magnetic—over the surface of the earth. This invisible wave or tide is said to operate in opposition to the earth's fields. This triggering is said to occur between September and February, bringing about an interaction between the earth's electric and magnetic fields and giving rise to short-lived phenomena—lasting up to ten minutes on the ocean floor and up to thirty minutes on the surface—such as ruptures or short circuits between these two fields or planes.

The result of this activity takes the form of invisible,

conical vortices of swirling magnetic fields of very high intensity. These volcano-like eruptions, it is claimed, cause a suction or attraction that can affect the ocean's surface in diameters reaching sixteen miles across, while spewing "white vapors" high into the atmosphere.

Both of these psychics believe that the center of the phenomenon lies southwest of Key West in the Florida Strait. Some of the triangle writers and investigators interpret this as further support for the Atlantean theories, since this location is believed to have been part of the sunken continent of Atlantis. They suggest that the present islands in that area may have been mountaintops before the continent sank into the ocean.

Although no pyramids have yet been found on the bottom of Lake Ontario, there are other ways in which this region parallels, if not surpasses, the Bermuda Triangle.

As shown earlier, this lake is subjected to some very sudden and violent storms, which burst upon ships with unexpected speed. Occurring in such a limited area as this lake, storm-generated infrasound might be of a shorter duration and the effects swifter and far more disastrous than on an open ocean. Was it the so-called "voice of the sea" sweeping across this lake that battered the ten-thousand-ton *Protostatis* into scrap?

Whatever it was, it had an unbelievable power capable of buckling over a hundred of her steel plates. Also, if it had been simply due to known storm phenomenon, or the infrasound suggested by the Russian theorists, it might be expected that the unleashed forces would have expended themselves during the first encounter with this freighter. However, this did not seem to be the case. In fact, the *Protostatis* appeared to have been pursued relentlessly and attacked three times.

The invisible forces discovered by the two Dutch psychics may offer a partial solution to some of the unexplained events taking place in the Great Lakes region. Also, the discovery of the columns of reduced binding by the Canadian research team under Wilbert B. Smith in the 1950s may prove to be eruptions of a similar nature. These pillar-like zones of reduced binding, however, were said to be only a thousand feet across, compared to those which the Dutch psychics claimed were sixteen miles in diameter. This smaller size may indicate a different strength of eruption for different latitudes. And this in turn brings to mind Smith's belief that the binding forces were stronger in the north and weaker in the south. Another approach to this difference might be that Smith had only detected the inner core of the forces while the Dutch psychics detected the overall field of radiation.

The method used by the Dutch psychics is a variation of the ancient practice of dowsing. This can be done with either a pendulum, a forked stick, or other type of dowsing index. In operation, the dowsing instrument is moved across a map, a chart, or even a hand drawn sketch representing the area to be dowsed. If the dowser is highly gifted, or sensitive, not only will the instrument be triggered at the appropriate location, but also the mind of the dowser will be supplied intuitively with further information concerning the location.

Records show that dowsing has been practiced for thousands of years and was known and used by the earliest of civilizations. It has been used to locate minerals, freshwater, and even favorable sites on which to establish settlements. Today it is being used to help locate mineral resources and to pinpoint archaeological sites.

No one knows exactly how dowsing works, and there are a variety of theories on the subject. Some believe it to be a method of contacting the spirit world from which the answers are supplied. Others believe it is a natural method of tuning into a universal data bank in which all information is stored. The most common explanation is that the forces or energies being detected by the dowser are being radiated by the material being sought, and it is these that the dowser's mind detects. How these radiations can be detected at a distance of thousands of miles is a question still to be answered.

The majority of dowsers agree that the dowsing instrument, be it a rod, wand, or pendulum, has no power in itself. It is merely a BPR—biophysical response—amplifier that is actuated unconsciously by messages coupled through a mind-muscle link and serves only to give a visual indication to the dowser. Information pertaining to the type of material or its distance from the dowser is retained in the mind and supplied to the consciousness of the dowser as intuitive knowledge.

Whether or not one or the other of these beliefs is correct seems to make little difference to the dowsers. Their past successes are testaments to the validity of their art.

Science as a whole does not share this belief in dowsing. This is particularly true of most Western scientists. However, dowsing has received considerable support from many scientists in Russia in the past decade. Professor Alexander Bakirov, head of the mineralogy department at the Tomsk Polytechnical Institute, has encouraged the setting up of a course in dowsing as part of the advanced curriculum at the departments of geology and geophysics at the Moscow State University. Dr. A. A. Ogilvy, chairman of the department of geology there, has supported the recommendation. At a seminar on the biophysical response method—the Russian term for dowsing—delegates were shown proof that dowsing before drilling for various ores had reduced the required drilling by 30 to 40 percent.

Among those in the Western societies who have shown a willingness to make use of this ancient art are members of the archaeological community. Dr. Norman Emerson, head of the University of Toronto's archaeology section, had considerable success using dowsers to aid in locating and charting out various archaeological sites, some even before any preliminary investigations had begun.

The same open-minded approach was demonstrated by the United States Marine Corps. According to the marines trained to use it, dowsing surpassed expensive electronic equipment in detecting underground tunnels, land mines, and munitions dumps. Unlike established science, the military authorities were willing to use an unconventional technique to get the job done.

In November 1975, Bob Ater, a noted Maine dowser, set to work to dowse a map of Lake Ontario at my request. His past successes in map dowsing include finding underground sources of water, lost items, and even two hikers who were lost in the White Mountain area of New Hampshire during an April snowstorm in 1975. Using a ballpoint pen and a map of the White Mountain area, he was able to direct the search party to the location where the lost hikers had taken shelter. His reward was a commendation from one of the staff at the Mount Washington Observatory and the gratitude of the lost hikers.

When Bob used the same technique on the map of Lake

Ontario his drawings appeared similar to what the Dutch psychics would describe two years later. At various places he drew in wavering lines of what he felt were natural flows of energy crossing the lake and wandering across the land on either side. Between these lines he drew in vortices of swirling energy of a different sort, which he felt displaced the natural flows. At other locations he marked in other eruptions and

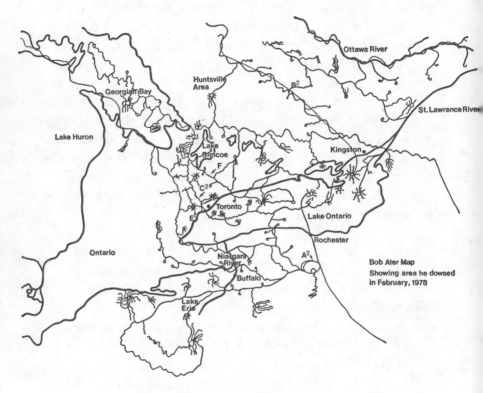

A²—termination of very large vortex. B²—very active area of emissions. C²—fault activity ending in Lake Ontario. D and E—areas of strange activity. F—fault.

Little "spiders" indicate areas of energy eruptions. The lines between "spiders" are energy flows through the earth.

these appear to radiate outward like fine tentacles. At a number of the locations where he drew loops in the lines he felt were natural flows, the loops matched closely the positions given for magnetic anomalies. These give the impression of being interruptions in the natural flows. Many of his locations that have swirling vortices seem to correspond to known faults or fracture zones. Curiously, UFO investigators and writers like John Keel have noticed a close relationship between these geologic features and UFO sightings.

What is most important is that Bob Ater marked out areas where he sensed strong emissions, and these closely matched the scenes where ship and plane "accidents" have occurred over the years.

Since this first experiment, Bob has provided me with other more detailed maps of this region. One he completed in the summer of 1977 covered the western end of Lake Ontario. This one indicated strong emissions along a north-south line extending from Lake Ontario north to the Georgian Bay, passing to the west of Toronto. As stated earlier (see page 10), in November of that year Tom Walker flew into a fog and was lost for two days; Craig Carlisle vanished in his aircraft at the Lake Ontario end in December; and it was north of this line that Gavine and Lind went missing in October. Further, during March 1978, almost two dozen sightings of UFOs were reported along this same area. All of these occurred in a corridor following the line marked out by Bob Ater.

Is this just coincidence?

Malva Dee is a Canadian psychic living at West Guilford, Ontario, about eighty miles north of the lake. Her specialty is psychometry, which is defined as the paranormal ability to ob-

tain facts from an object about its history or events connected
with it. When I asked her if she psychically sensed anything
unusual about the Lake Ontario region in general, she re-
plied: ". . . it just seems that there is a negative force field
here [in the southeast end of the lake] that extends into the
ether, that affects the living conditions in this particular section." She then went on to add: "It is just as if this portion of
the country were touched with some very strong radiation
force, which still lingers, so that as an aftermath of radiation,
nothing flourishes here as it should."

Is it this same negative force that Bob Ater detects when
he charts out the emissions in this area? Was it these forces
Captain James Richardson sensed when he warned of the dire
fate awaiting the *Speedy* on the night she vanished? Was it a
foreknowledge of erupting energies that caused the crew of
the *Eleanor Hamilton* to ask the captain to cancel the voyage
out on the lake?

The ability to detect invisible emissions coming from the
earth is not a new art in North America. At one time it was a
well-established profession among the Indian inhabitants, and
it was one of the services performed by the Miday priests or
medicine men. It was the method used to select sites for villages or hunting grounds because it was believed that certain
areas were free of harmful emissions, and these "clean" areas
were thought to be conducive to the good health and well-be-
ing of the tribe. Such sites were thought to have been chosen
by the god or deity, and this information was passed on to the
medicine men while they were in contact with the gods or de-
mons during trance states.

Among the methods used to make this contact was a ceremony known as the "shaking tent." The site for this ritual

was chosen by the medicine man who dowsed the area until he located a spot where he sensed a column of energy rising up out of the earth. Over this spot a wigwam was constructed, using seven pine poles set firmly into the earth and their tops lashed together. Beaver hides were then used to cover the frame, leaving one opening at the apex where the poles protruded and one for the doorway. When the ceremony began, the medicine man stripped himself naked, entered the tent, and threw himself prone on the earthen floor, then the doorway of hides was closed. Outside, members of the tribe sat in a circle surrounding the tent while the medicine man began the chant that would put him into a trance.

As soon as contact was made with the deities, the whole tent was said to vibrate and shudder, its motions becoming more violent until the jolting and swaying threatened to bring the tent crashing to the ground. At this point bright sparks and strange lights are said to have appeared over the apex of the tent, and this announced the arrival of the spirits. Amid eerie wailing and loud drumming coming from inside the tent, the moans of the medicine man would be heard as his spirit left his body and rose up to the top of the tent. Here it is said to have floated until communication with the spirits was completed, then it returned to his body.

Probably the first European to witness this strange ceremony was Father Lejeune, a Catholic missionary. His eyewitness account of the event was recorded in his *Relations* for the year 1634. To this early missionary, the whole ritual was a pagan event in which savages were attempting to invoke the forces of evil.

Somewhat more vivid accounts were written in later years when trappers, traders, and mounted police witnessed the ceremony. In the book *Exploring the Supernatural*, R. S. Lambert revealed some of the actions taken by skeptical white witnesses. Most refused to believe that the tent was being shaken by invisible forces. Some tried to hold the poles down and had them pulled from their grasp by superhuman powers whose energies whirled in a cyclonic force around the inside of the tent. Others cut the tent open only to find the body of the medicine man lying limp on the floor. After the ritual was over these skeptics were even more puzzled to find that, although the tent had leaped violently back and forth, even bending toward the ground, the seven poles were still solidly anchored in the ground and they were unable to pull them free!

Exactly what method the medicine man used to invoke these forces is something that appears to have been forgotten over the years, and the practice has been outlawed by most tribes. According to Father Lejeune, who stated that he questioned the medicine man about the appearance of the spirits that had entered the tent, these spirits were described as being much larger than a man's fist and they possessed long tapered tails. When the missionary asked if that meant the spirits were cone-shaped, he was told they were. When he asked about the brilliant sparks and weird lights seen above the tent, he was told they came from the spirits.

If these spirits, or conic vortices, that appeared inside the tent are smaller versions of the larger swirling vortices being described by the psychics, then it would be interesting to know just how they can be commanded to appear. Since the medicine man is said to have entered the tent naked, we might assume that the only tool he had available for attracting these invisible vortices was the power of his mind. Barring that, since the medicine man chose the site for the ritual, possibly he hid something in the ground at the site beforehand. But what?

One of the early North American Indian beliefs is that there are places on the earth where these energies come to the surface. At these points the energy emerges in a straight line connecting the two lower worlds with the earth's surface and the three heavens above the earth. If such lines of emerging energy exist, then the medicine man, by positioning himself directly over this line or within its field, may have allowed the energies or their vibrations to act as an aid for inducing a trance state through which he received information he sought for the tribe. This, however, does not explain what caused the tent to shake violently and the strange lights to appear.

These beliefs in erupting energies parallel similar beliefs in other ancient cultures around the world. They appear to be the basis of the theories of telluric, or earth, currents and ley lines. Some of the radiations coming from these were thought to be an aid to human health while others were detrimental to the physical body. In many parts of Britain and Europe, these invisible rivers of energy are said to be marked out by the huge stones and dolmens such as those found at Karnac in France.

These lines of energy were believed to surround the earth much like the magnetic lines of force, yet were somehow confined to channels that routed them on north-south or east-west flows. At times it would appear that certain conditions would interrupt these flows, giving rise to diversions just as a river is diverted around an island. At certain points on the earth it was believed that these flows were drawn down into the earth, while at others they would loop up into the atmosphere in nodes where they became mixed with what sometimes was called "raw" energy of a type unsuitable to humans.

Intersections also seemed to be considered very important. At points where these flows crossed at right angles, huge dolmens or stone circles were constructed to mark these sites. Paul Bouchet, a Grand Druid of the Druidic priesthood of France, a group supporting these ancient beliefs, suggests that wherever the currents within the earth's crust meet a water current, a menhir was erected and, if the flow was split into two or more branches, dolmens with two or more supports were erected to indicate the number of branches. At many of these locations, altars and places of worship were said to have been established so that inhabitants of the area could gather to receive a sort of resonance by being immersed in this outflow of energy.

Thomas E. Ross of Pennsylvania has taken a great interest in the ancient belief in ley lines. In a personal communication, he told me he believes that the triangles or zones of mystery are closely related to eruptions of rogue ley lines. These, he states, are lines of energy emerging from the earth which have not been stripped of their terrestrial energy by contact with a surface line of solar energy. He goes on to explain that in most areas the energy flows emerging from the earth and the lines of solar energy are aligned in their contact with each other. However, at the so-called triangle zones this alignment does not exist, and the effect is an unbalance of energy in the atmosphere. He suggests that it is these unstripped energies that bring about the problems such as those encountered by the freighter *Protostatis* and the other ships and planes.

This theory appears similar to those put forward by the two Dutch psychics, Croiset and Tholen, and those of Malva Dee and Bob Ater. Basically, all are suggesting strong emissions from the earth.

While there is evidence on which to theorize that there are powerful forces being generated inside the earth by some natural phenomenon that could cause these eruptions or emissions, other evidence seems to indicate that these eruptions may be triggered by other forces outside the earth's sphere. Some investigators, such as the two Dutch psychics, have suggested this. They proposed a sort of magnetic tide caused by the passage of the moon.

In the book, *Space-Time Transients & Unusual Events*, Drs. M. A. Persinger and G. F. Lafrenière, of Laurentian University in Ontario, Canada, proposed that certain solar and lunar occurrences trigger geomagnetic and atmospheric anomalies and these can be time correlated to Fortean events in susceptible areas and may prove to be the mechanism bringing about such episodes. They go on to state that recent information gathered by satellite reconnaissance has provided data to support this relationship.

Any such forces, whether from inside the earth or from outside, should be gravitational or electromagnetic-like in nature. If they are the latter, then their vibrations or frequencies of operation should be detectable on some portion of the frequency spectrum. So far, no such forces have been discovered that can be shown to be capable of causing a huge freighter or aircraft to vanish suddenly. However, there are some well-founded theories that propose that all matter, including living matter, is basically energy in motion and is thus susceptible to strong electrical influences from outside sources.

For years psychics have tried to point out to scientists that there are undiscovered invisible forces—basically electrical—at work all around us. Those psychics, who have developed the ability to see auras—electrical fields—that exist around humans and animals and even around nonliving objects, have described these as a maze of energy fields and forces. They describe these fields as fluorescent-like shells made up of fine lines of flowing energy. Among these are flares like vortices that seem to emerge from a central point in the body while other lines of energy appear to be drawn from an outside source.

In humans the strength and intensity of these glowing fields appear linked to physical and emotional conditions; and some appear to be under the control of the mind and can be willed to increase and decrease in strength.

Strangest of all are the fields and lines of energy seen surrounding mineral crystals. Psychics able to see these describe them as fine lines of light and a glowing radiance that forms looping and whirling spirals; others are like cones in which the energies appear as steady flows or pulsing, rhythmic waves. Even in these nonliving crystals the psychics see energy being drawn in from an outside source, while another sort of energy surges out from a central point inside the crystal and loops before darting back in.

If we were to apply the findings of these psychics to the material world around us, then we might expect that all of the minerals that go to make up the earth, which in themselves possess a crystalline lattice, should also radiate fields and lines of energy. Such a concept could also mean that large deposits of ore inside the earth would radiate combined fields and energies large enough to permeate the atmosphere above them. The interactions between these and the fields said to exist around plants would make the surface of the earth a veritable jungle of invisible energies and forces. Add to these the fields and forces said to be propagated over the earth by the passage of the moon or the movements of the planets, and the picture becomes an astounding ocean of energies. In the midst of this turmoil, the human brain with its own intricate electrical system might easily be subjected to a flood of energies that could overload or distort normal patterns of behavior. Are these the cause of so-called moon madness? Is this why certain ancient societies sought out locations on the earth where the emissions were said to be in harmony with the human body? Is this why places such as Lourdes in France, Holy Hill outside Milwaukee, and similar sites are noted for their healings and cures?

If this is the case, then the present scientific list of energies is far from complete.

# 6 Other Zones of Mystery

If an entire ancient city were discovered beneath the Bermuda Triangle, there would be little doubt in the minds of many people that it would prove to be the remains of Atlantis. Archaeologists, however, would require time to make a thorough study of the ruins before they could pass judgment or make claims.

The conditions in the Lake Ontario region are somewhat different. Here there are no popular legends, but there are ruins of an ancient *something*. These are situated on dry land and appear to be of historical significance, but no recognized archaeologist will examine them.

This may seem a paradox, but it is a fact that the stone ruins scattered through the bush two hundred odd miles to the east of Lake Ontario have been known to local people since the time the area was first settled. They are in an area that is relatively accessible and yet no full-scale archaeological investigation has ever been carried out. According to the few experts who have casually looked into these mysterious ruins, the structures are nothing more than crude colonial animal pens. Amateur archaeologists who have worked on the sites refuse to accept this answer, and the enigma of the stone ruins remains unresolved.

There are over two hundred of these mysterious stone structures. They are located in numerous places all the way from New England to New York and New Jersey. They include twenty-six-foot-high towers, so-called tombs and sacrificial tables, and long walls that measure six feet wide and four feet high. Some of the huge stones appear to have been erected for astronomical purposes, others to mark boundaries.

Probably the greatest collection of ruins lie within the boundaries of "Mystery Hill," a privately owned area just off Route 111 outside North Salem, New Hampshire. The owner, Robert Stone, has formed a group of amateur archaeologists into an organization dedicated to preserving the site and gathering information of possible importance concerning the ruins.

No exact dates have been established for these ruins, and it is still unknown who the builders were. Some artifacts have been carbon-dated and show that the site was in use some four thousand years ago. Several theories have been put forth to show that the original builders were Vikings who arrived in the area almost four hundred years before Columbus; others offer equally valid proof that the area was occupied by Phoenicians before the Christian era.

Among those offering solutions to the mystery is a Harvard professor of biology, H. Barraclough (Barry) Fell. In his book *America B.C.*, Barry Fell suggests that the inscriptions found at many of the sites are Phoenician, Iberian, Punic, and Celtic Ogham. He further suggests that the combination of these arose from the fusion of cultures on the Iberian peninsula before 1000 B.C. and was brought to the site by the early settlers from that area.

Fell's opponents stop short of calling him mad. Some say that the tablets and stones on which the inscriptions appear are questionable, even frauds. Even so, there are those within the professions who offer Fell support. Among them is a Vermont astronomer, Byron Dix, who has independently found evidence of alignments that suggest some astronomical function for some of Fell's sites.

In 1820, at a point fifteen miles south of Lake Ontario, just outside Palmyra, New York, the details of a similar ancient society were revealed to a fourteen-year-old farm boy. The boy's name was Joseph Smith and he had gone into the bush near his father's farm to meditate. As he sat thinking, he became aware of a thick darkness that was creeping in around him. In a short time he found himself paralyzed and a fear began to grip him. When he thought he was about to die he began to pray, then he looked up and saw a column of light descending from the sky above him. When the light touched him, it seemed to release him from the grip of the darkness, and he looked with astonishment at the two beings in shining robes that appeared with the light.

The two figures seemed suspended in the column above Smith and one of the figures pointed at the other, then a voice said: "This is my son. Hear him."

Smith's astonishment held him rooted to the spot. Later he said that the speaker identified himself as Mormon, the historian of the Nephites, the first civilization established in North America in ancient times. He was then informed that the being with him was his son, Moroni, the one who would visit Smith again over the next few years. With that, the column of light withdrew into the sky and Smith was left to puzzle the meaning of it all.

In Smith's testimony concerning this event, he tells that the beings informed him that he had been chosen for an important task: He was to interpret the writings in a book of gold pages that had belonged to the ancient inhabitants of North America.

In 1823, three years later, Moroni returned to explain the mission to Smith. In this second visit, Moroni again appeared in a column of light that filled Smith's bedroom, and before he left he provided him with a vision of the book of gold pages, which he said would be found in a stone vault with a rounded top, buried in the highest hill in the area.

Smith visited this hill the following day and located the stone vault, but it was another four years before he was permitted to open the vault to see the book. During these years Moroni continued to visit Smith in order to prepare him for the task of translating the writings in the book of gold pages.

When the time finally came, Smith was able to remove the book and begin the work. To aid him in this, the vault also contained a breastplate with two stones in silver bows fastened to it. These stones constituted the Urim and Thummim, which were said to have the power to aid in understanding, and to provide knowledge of right and wrong. Also helping with the work were several of Smith's close friends who later signed a document stating that they had seen and handled this book of gold pages. When the task was completed, the book was returned to the vault and the vault closed.

This translation became the *Book of Mormon* and it contained the history of the Nephite civilization. It reveals a complex tale of a group of people who migrated to North America and eventually became divided into two groups, the

Nephites and Lamanites, who warred against each other. In A.D. 385 they met in a final great battle on Hill Cumora, a few miles south of what is now Palmyra, New York. In this the Nephites reportedly were wiped out and the Lamanites—said to have been the ancestors of the North American Indians—took over all of the continent.

Smith went on to establish the Church of Jesus Christ of the Latter-Day Saints, more commonly called the Mormon Church. But he never lived to see it prosper. Religious intolerance was rampant, and in 1844 he was jailed at Carthage, Illinois, and while awaiting trial was taken out and shot by an armed mob.

According to the texts that Smith translated, the Nephites were supposed to have been a prosperous civilization. Their society spread out across the continent and included many great cities. Whether these were the cities of light spoken of in the Indian legends is not known. However, the story ties in closely with these legends and also those told of the city of Saganna where men flew like birds.

If such an ancient Nephite race did live in this area, it is doubtful if every last one was wiped out in the final battle. A small group may have survived. It is also possible that such survivors went on to become the ancestors of the strange tribe that Cartier found living on the St. Lawrence River. It might also explain why this St. Lawrence tribe built its villages in pyramid fashion. Such a style could have been a carry-over from earlier times when their race had built great cities and temples. Finally, it might also explain the cultural differences existing between this tribe and their neighbors.

The revelations made by Smith, and the interpretations being applied to the ancient ruins east of Lake Ontario, add new elements to the already strange history of this region. But more than strangeness will be required to provide the stimulus that will attract scientific attention. Something along this line may be forthcoming. Early in 1977 the magazine *Beyond Reality* published a small item from the Woodstock *Times* in Woodstock, New York. The item concerned the work of a scientific team under Dr. Carl Metcalfe which was carrying out investigations on ruins in the Devil's Tombstone area. According to the article the exact location of this archaeological work was being kept secret lest vandals interrupt the work. However, it was revealed that the team had uncovered what may turn out to be the most important find ever made in that area. This consisted of some priceless artifacts, among them a gold tablet on a giant block of granite!

The article made no mention of any writing on the tablet, only that the artifacts appeared to show traces of Mayan influence. Since then, no more has been heard of this team or its discoveries. If the find proves genuine it might provide a link with Joseph Smith's claim of an ancient race that inhabited this region of the continent. Any discoveries supporting this belief are sure to be controversial since proof of Smith's claims would open the door to a flood of evidence which might prove the so-called Indian legends to be a true history.

Smith was not the only one in this area to become involved with beings from out of the past. In Hydesville, New York, a short distance east of the site where Smith had his encounter with Mormon and Moroni, two sisters, Margarette and Catherine Fox, became curious about strange rapping sounds coming from the walls and doors of their home. At the time, Margarette was fifteen and Catherine was twelve—Joseph Smith had been fourteen at the time of his first encounter—and statistics show this to be the age range in which the majority of people are likely to encounter or develop their psychic abilities. Thus it is not surprising that the two girls soon discovered that by asking questions requiring yes or no answers, the knocks would respond accordingly—one rap for yes, a double rap for no. News of this psychic activity spread and so astounded residents in the area that the girls' parents tried to put an end to the communications. They decided to separate the sisters, sending them to live with relatives in nearby towns, but the question-and-answer rappings continued even in the other homes.

This contact with spirits from another world brought about the beginning of modern spiritualism and the fame of the two sisters even reached Europe. Requests came from highly placed persons seeking their help in getting answers to important questions, and the sisters soon found themselves in demand on both continents.

The most astounding information the Fox sisters received concerned a murder that had taken place in the Fox home prior to their father's purchase of the house. This revelation led to the discovery of the remains of a body buried in one corner of the cellar. Evidence found with the remains proved that the information was correct: There had been a murder. However, the spirits would not reveal the murderer's identity.

With the discovery of this body, the fame of the sisters reached even greater heights and spiritualism became a parlor fad that reached even the White House, where it was used as a form of after-dinner entertainment by Mary Todd Lincoln, the President's wife.

Among those investigating psychic phenomena, there are many who feel that certain areas of the earth are conducive to the psychic development of individuals. Whether this development is due to radiations emerging from the earth, and immersing the physical body in fields that trigger little-known mechanisms in the human brain, is not known, simply because such a phenomenon has never been thoroughly investigated.

If there are bioelectric triggering forces erupting in particular locations, then this region of the Great Lakes must certainly be one of them. What could be offered as further proof of this is the case of Daniel Dunglas Home. Home's parents were Scottish immigrants who arrived in eastern New York State while he was still quite young. They took up farming near Albany, and by the time he had reached his teens he was also developing his psychic abilities. In 1848 he reached the age of fifteen, (the same year in which the Fox sisters, also in their mid-teens, began experimenting with spiritualism). At twenty-two he traveled to Europe to demonstrate his abilities, and before he died was a close friend of Catherine Fox, then Mrs. Jencken, and on intimate terms with most of Europe's monarchs.

Among Home's accomplishments was the ability to levitate himself off the ground. He demonstrated this repeatedly while under close observation by noted scientists of that time, and on one occasion floated himself out of a hotel window and entered through another. His other abilities included handling live coals—even inducing others to handle them—without harm. He could move objects at a distance and astounded observers by causing an accordion to play while it was locked inside a steel cage.

Sir William Crookes, the noted English physicist, tested Home's abilities under laboratory conditions numerous times and declared them genuine and without fraud. But when

Home died in 1886 at the age of fifty-three, he left behind more disbelievers than believers.

In the quarter of a century between the 1820s and 1848, Smith, Home, and the Fox sisters shredded a portion of the curtain of reality woven by nineteenth-century science. They left a legacy of doubt about our concepts of the material world, and those doubts still linger today.

Is the amazing psychic development of these people evidence of unknown forces and fields that erupt in this area and intrude on the workings of the human mind? Are these the same forces that penetrate the minds of seamen and pilots and cause them to run their vessels aground and crash their aircraft? There is certainly something operating here, and it has been producing bizarre and frightening events for a very long time.

On December 9, 1891, the residents of the small town of Lyons, New York, a short distance from Palmyra, observed a bright light in the night sky that lit up the whole area with an eerie blue glow. For almost three quarters of an hour it persisted, and observers who witnessed the phenomenon described it as a blue-white aurora-like glow that remained over the town and periodically increased in intensity, although no source of light could be detected.

During the first four months of 1892, the same blue-white glow appeared each evening, then it would fade away, leaving the residents of Lyons to wonder what was causing the strange atmospheric display.

The phenomenon was reported to local authorities, but no explanation was ever offered. As in the case of the mysterious "aircraft" that had shone brilliant searchlights on towns along the St. Lawrence, officialdom remained strangely silent.

One witness, Dr. M. A. Veeder, wrote his observations in an article for the May 1892 issue of *Scientific American*. Yet this produced no investigations or explanations. In the end, the glow over Lyons disappeared and so did the concern and interest in the subject. This simple vanishing act has repeatedly saved the so-called experts the embarrassment of not having an answer. When the phenomenon is gone, there is nothing left to investigate.

The event that took place at Popular Plains, New York, on November 12, 1966, certainly left something to investigate. It began in the early morning darkness when a strange light illuminated the sky, then was immediately accompanied by a thunderous explosion.

Residents at first thought the light and the explosion were the result of a meteorite plunging into the atmosphere. This seemed the most plausible explanation because a large crater was discovered in the field of a nearby farm. But when the crater was thoroughly examined, no fragments could be found to support this theory.

This event remained a mystery, although several experts were brought in to find out if the crater had been blasted out by explosives or a pocket of gas seeping up through the soil. However, no evidence was found to support even these theories.

A further element was added to the mystery when on November 12, 1967, another thunderous explosion and flash shook the area and lit the sky. Again, a crater was found just a few yards from the previous blast.

This time the military were brought into the investigation along with the FBI. Again the site was thoroughly examined and soil samples were taken for laboratory analysis. But the tests failed to find evidence to show that the holes had been blasted out by explosives. Nor did metal detectors or radiation counters reveal anything unusual in the craters.

And then, on November 12, 1968, a third explosion rocked the area and a brilliant flash of light lit up the sky. Again a crater was found by the stunned residents and it, too, was within a few yards of the previous blasts.

Once more the authorities and scientists were brought into the area and another thorough search was made. Needless to say, nothing was learned from the investigation.

For the next few years the inhabitants of the area kept a watch to see if the phenomenon would be repeated on November 12. So far, all has been quiet at Popular Plains and this has brought the hope that the phenomenon has moved elsewhere.

The site of these explosions is about forty miles east and south of Palmyra. This puts it inside a zone or corridor that passes across the continent from the Atlantic Ocean to a point west of Chicago. Along this corridor, mysterious events have occurred that defy explanation. The only thing they appear to have in common is an association with Lake Ontario or one of the other Great Lakes. Something in this area seems to attract weird phenomena. Or they are the result of the interactions of little-known energies such as those said to have been known to ancient societies.

In Jay Gourley's book, *The Great Lakes Triangle,* he listed an astonishing number of documented aircraft losses that occurred in this region over the past years. Many of these planes vanished or crashed in ways that defy explanation. But what is more important is that the majority of these aircraft "accidents" have taken place in clusters along the corridor described above. Most of them happened in the section of this corridor between mid-New York State and Chicago. If this is coincidence, then it is a coincidence as astounding as the case of TWA Flight 841.

On the evening of April 4, 1979, Captain Harvey Gibson entered the corridor over Lake Erie, south of Buffalo, on a scheduled nonstop flight from New York to Minneapolis. The plane was a three-engine Boeing 727, said to be one of the most reliable airplanes ever built. At about 10 P.M. the plane passed Flint, Michigan, cruising at thirty-nine thousand feet in clear weather. Until that point, the flight had been routine. Then the plane suddenly began to vibrate, did a 360-degree barrel roll, and went into a plunge toward the earth that took it down five miles at supersonic speed and almost ended in complete disaster!

Luckily, at twelve thousand feet the pilot lowered the landing gear in an attempt to abort the plunge, and the maneuver brought the plane out of the dive. Minutes later he was able to make a bumpy emergency landing at Detroit, where it was discovered that a wing and the landing gear had been damaged during the event.

George Weiss, an astounded spokesman for Boeing, told reporters, "We've never had anything like this before." According to Langhorne Bond, head of the Federal Aviation Administration, it was a miracle that the plane held together. "I can't think of another incident where a [commercial, passenger carrying] plane has done a complete 360-degree roll-over and survived," he told reporters.

Federal investigators learned from Captain Gibson that, just prior to the event, he had noticed that the autopilot was making hard corrections to the left as the plane began to yaw to the right. At that point Gibson had switched to manual control, but the plane continued the freak maneuver.

What puzzled federal investigators most was the plane's flight recorder tape, which contains the air crew's conversation. The tape was blank for the period during the unexplained event. Some of the investigators theorized that the maneuver was not a complete roll-over, but that the motions of the aircraft were so violent that it appeared to the crew that the ship had rolled 360 degrees.

Some investigators believe that the autopilot malfunctioned and brought on the whole event, but none can explain how. This brings us back to the earlier proposal that energies erupting in this region of the continent might be able to disrupt the delicate bioelectric systems of the human brain. If so, could they not also affect the equally sensitive electrical systems in an aircraft?

# 7 The Unexplained Objects

Of all the mysteries occurring in this and other regions, none are more perplexing than the unexplained objects that have been observed in the sky or sitting on the ground. In most cases they are described either as lights from an unknown source or as actual material objects. While there is evidence to indicate that many of them are the direct result of unknown natural forces, there is also evidence that these same forces are under intelligent control and are being used to achieve a specific purpose.

If this is outside intrusion through the control of natural forces, then the method involved could be compared with the way in which humans have learned to control electromagnetic forces for radio communication and television. In the latter case, humans are using a natural phenomenon for their own purposes. Likewise, it may be that there are other intelligences who can make use of the energies and forces of the earth for reasons of their own.

An example of this might be the way the *Speedy* vanished,

leaving the government of Upper Canada decimated. Another could be the way "unfavorable conditions" prevented any decisive action from taking place on Lake Ontario during the War of 1812.

More important would be the unexplained "development" of individuals as in the cases of Joseph Smith, the Fox sisters, and D. D. Home. Each appears to have been influenced or triggered in some way to develop special abilities that allowed them to introduce concepts that altered the world around them.

Was all of this just the hand of fate? Were these events brought about by an accidental encounter with invisible radiations or energy eruptions coming from the earth? Or is there some sort of intelligence working behind the scenes?

An examination of the so-called UFO phenomenon over the years tends to give the impression that there is some sort of outside intelligence at work. At these times the UFO seems to be an actual object or craft, possibly from another planet. Yet at other times it appears to be a natural earthbound phenomenon that has never been fully recognized as such, nor has ever been fully examined by science.

Either way, the Great Lakes region seems to have an abundant supply of them. Since the late 1960s there has been a dramatic upsurge in UFO sightings throughout this region, particularly in the nocturnal-light variety of UFO. The following cases demonstrate only a small portion of this activity.

Probably the first celestial object that catches the attention of most people is the moon. But it was not the moon that gripped the attention of a young couple around 9:30 P.M. on a mild August evening in 1965. Parked near a reservoir outside Ottawa, Ontario, they were startled by a brilliant light. When they looked up, they saw a glowing object descending toward the reservoir. On the underside were what appeared to be four searchlights, which were illuminating the whole area.

When the object got within twenty feet of the surface of the water, it halted and hovered. Something like a sliding door opened in the side of the craft, then moments later what appeared to be the figure of a man was framed in the opening. As the couple watched, two more figures appeared beside the first and all three seemed to be wearing clothing that had a metallic sheen.

At this point the woman became frightened and the couple fled without discovering what the object was or what the beings in the craft were up to.

The UFO investigators, who looked into this case and questioned the couple (who requested their names not be used), noted in their report that the site was near a quarry and that there were high-tension lines nearby. In many UFO sightings there seems to be some relationship between UFOs and power lines or quarries. Just what this relationship is has never been determined.

In August and again in October 1966, residents of New York State from Sodus, on the edge of Lake Ontario, to Port Gibson, twenty-five miles to the south, observed a brilliant light that hovered and moved about the area before heading northeast out over the lake. In one location the light was seen hovering for thirty minutes. During this time witnesses reported that the light oscillated, flashing red and green and white before the object moved off over the lake.

State police said, that during the sighting, reports began coming in around 8 P.M. and continued until 8:30 P.M.

It was dark at 2:30 A.M. on June 13, 1967, when Carmen Cuneo, a mine worker at Caledonia, Ontario, between Lake

Ontario and Lake Erie, stepped out of one of the Domtar Quarry buildings for a breath of fresh air. As he came out he caught sight of a thirty-six-foot-long cigar-shaped object close to the quarry floor and a fifteen-foot disk-shaped object hovering above it.

At first the mine worker was not sure what he was seeing as he looked at what appeared to be four evenly spaced windows along the side of the cigar-shaped object. He was even more puzzled when he spotted three small figures moving about as if collecting something from the ground. The figures appeared to be wearing bubble-like helmets with amber lights on top.

After staring at the strange sight for about ten minutes, he went back inside the building to get one of the other workers. They came out just in time to see the two objects rising into the air above the quarry, where they hovered for about twenty minutes before heading off to the southwest, flashing multicolored lights but making no sound.

Later on, when the sun had come up, the mine worker went to the place where the strange object had hovered and discovered an oil-like residue on the ground. When samples of the substance were tested they were found to be much like ordinary lubricating oil.

Around 5 A.M. on a dark morning in the middle of August 1967, a salesman—called Joe Edwards for reasons of privacy— driving along Highway 15 north of Kingston, Ontario, observed a huge glowing object giving off a brilliant green light as it descended from the sky. When it reached treetop height, it moved down the highway ahead of the salesman's car and disappeared around a bend in the road. Minutes later, as the man rounded the curve, he again caught sight of this strange object, which he described as being much like an inverted soup bowl sitting on three legs, in a field two hundred to three hundred yards from the highway.

As he neared the object he slowed down, pulled off onto the edge of the highway, and switched off the car's lights. For the next few minutes he sat stunned as he watched three small humanlike creatures, about three feet tall, as they moved about outside the object gathering up bits of soil and plants. They were dressed in white coveralls and wore bubble-type helmets on their heads.

After watching the activity for a few minutes the man switched the car lights on and put them on high beam, hoping to get a better look at the creatures. As he did so they hurried back to the large craft and immediately took off. Within seconds they were gone.

When the man reported the sighting to the local police, they told him they had already received a number of calls reporting a strange green light in the sky. When the police accompanied the salesman back to the site, they found burn marks on the ground and three indentations where something had touched down on the earth.

Around five-thirty that evening, the so-called landing site was examined by investigators from the United States Air Force who estimated that the indentations had been made under a pressure of a hundred thousand pounds.

These investigators questioned the salesman for over an hour. Before they left they advised him to say nothing to anyone about the incident and told him they would be in touch with him when they had completed their investigation. So far he has heard nothing.

At 10:30 P.M. on June 17, 1968, James Bryers, an alderman for Scarborough, Ontario, and his wife stepped from their car in their driveway in time to see a huge orange globe of light

pass over their house just above treetop height. During the
five minutes they watched this object, it seemed to be breaking up, and bright orange chunks appeared to fly off. These
chunks would glow brightly, vanish, then reappear, still glowing, only to vanish again seconds later.

The Bryers home is within a few hundred yards of the edge
of Scarborough Bluffs on the shore of Lake Ontario. The object moved forward, paused to hover and rise, then moved
ahead again as it followed the edge of the bluffs and finally
disappeared in the distance.

The couple entered the house at ten forty-five and their
son, who had been watching from a window, spotted a second
glowing orange object coming from the east on the same
course as the first, but at a slightly higher altitude. As it
repeated the maneuvers of the first object, the couple and
their son had an opportunity to compare it with a commercial
aircraft that flew overhead. Although the plane was at a much
higher altitude, the couple felt that the pilot must have seen
the brilliant object because there was no moon in the sky.
However, no such confirmation was received when they contacted the Toronto International Airport. This second sighting lasted for approximately five minutes before the object
disappeared over the lake.

By eleven-twenty the Bryers had put the matter aside for
the time being and had settled down in their living room to
finish off some paperwork related to their business. Within
minutes the alderman's wife called out as she glanced out the
window and saw a third glowing object coming from the
same direction.

This one was even lower than the first two—almost at treetop height. It was also huge compared to the first two. The
alderman estimated that this one measured two to three

inches on a ruler held at arm's length, and at this time the object was approximately a mile away. This would make the object over one hundred feet across.

Taking his binoculars, the alderman ran to the backyard and climbed on a three-foot wall for a better look. However, the object was moving faster, and he was only able to hold it in view for three to four seconds before it passed by and went below the level of the trees.

Alerting one of his neighbors and telling him there was a UFO over his house, Bryers ran to the end of the street near the bluffs where he was joined by two teenagers, who had also been watching the objects. From then until it was completely lost from view, the trio took turns watching the object through the binoculars.

This third object was described as being very round, large, and flat. The underside appeared to have a central hub and spokes, which appeared dark against the rest of the craft. It was giving off an intense yellow-orange color that seemed to be coming from inside the object. It was also noted that the bright glow did not reflect on the rooftops or trees as the UFO passed over. Nor did it pause to hover and rise as did the first two. None of these objects made any sounds and none had any signs of clearance lights, which conventional aircraft have.

All told, some twenty individuals witnessed these strange globes of light. Their agreement on what they saw rules out any suggestion of imagination on the part of the witnesses.

In a communication from Mr. Bryers in January 1978, I was told that he had been contacted by the U.S. military with a request for a complete report on the sightings. This was followed by a similar request from Canadian military authorities. In both cases he was assured he would be contacted after the investigations had been completed. To this date, ten years later, Mr. Bryers had heard nothing from them.

On the evening of September 12, 1969, Robert McConkie, a high school teacher on holiday, watched a brightly glowing object as it crossed the sky toward Rice Lake, twelve miles north of Lake Ontario. The object came down in the lake near a small island and continued to glow brightly for about two minutes, then vanished for two minutes, then reappeared and glowed brightly for another five minutes.

The high school teacher stated that the object did not glide in, as an aircraft might do in an emergency landing. Instead, it came straight down and splashed into the water.

The object had glowed like something on fire, and this caused the teacher to become concerned enough to phone the local police, telling them he would go out and investigate. Strangely, the police did not investigate the matter themselves, although there was the possibility that such an event might have been a plane crashing into the lake. When queried about this lack of interest, the police glibly told a reporter from a local paper that, since they had heard nothing more from the teacher, they assumed he had been kidnapped by the little green men from the glowing object.

It was later learned that the teacher had gone out to the site accompanied by a local resort owner, but their search of the water around the small island had failed to turn up any evidence as to what the glowing object had been. Whatever it was, it had simply vanished.

Around 7 P.M. December 10, 1969, the sky was clear enough for the pilot of a light aircraft flying across Lake Ontario to see the lights of Kingston 170 miles to the east. He was flying at an altitude of three thousand feet and was midpoint in his flight from St. Catharines, Ontario, to Toronto Island Airport, when he noticed a bright light hovering close to the lake. The light was white and appeared to oscillate up and down with no side movement. When the pilot contacted Toronto radar, he was informed that they were not picking up a blip in that sector, but he continued to watch the light for ten minutes.

A few minutes later another small plane came into the area, and its pilot also reported the bright white light, which he watched for five minutes. At that point the light ceased oscillating and disappeared to the southeast at a very high rate of speed.

When local UFO investigators learned of the incident, they checked and found that no weather balloons had been released in that area, nor were there any other aircraft aside from those mentioned.

About seventy-five miles due north of Lake Ontario lies Boshkung Lake. One evening in November 1973, Earl Pitts and Jim Cooper, two local real estate agents, were driving by the lake and were stunned when they saw a huge cone-shaped object in the cool November sky. They described it as having a bright glow at the front and rear, and it moved rapidly from west to east. They were not the only ones to see this object. Dale Parnell, a private pilot, and his wife were driving along a highway farther east of this point and they, too, observed the glowing object. They described it as a "huge and awesome sight."

Another resident living close to Boshkung Lake later reported seeing an object described as being like a helicopter with no tail. This one passed down a small valley at treetop height as it headed toward the lake. On the bottom of this object there appeared to be four landing struts partly raised, and the top of the object was lit up and glowing.

For the next few months this area became a hotbed for UFO sightings. One resident claimed that hardly a night passed without the brilliant glowing objects making an appearance. They came in all shapes, including a cigar-shaped craft and some shaped like pollywogs. They came in reds and blacks, some with multiple flashing lights, arriving in the area of the lake singly or in pairs, usually around sundown. At times during the winter, the ice on the lake took on the appearance of a science-fiction space port!

When the Ontario Provincial Police were called in to investigate the situation, they stated that the objects were only reflections, but did not explain what they were reflections of. When the police left the scene, the "reflections" zoomed up into the sky! When the local residents reported this strange occurrence to the Department of Defence, they were met with the same bland indifference.

By February 1974, the objects, which had now become a nuisance to residents, grew bolder and moved in closer to the homes around the lake. One came within forty feet of one home and the object appeared to be having trouble trying to get off the ground.

Throughout this weird display the residents noted that whenever the objects were around the area, their television sets acted up and stations faded out.

By March, a reporter for the Minden *Progress*, the local newspaper, described his five-night vigil on the lake which ended when a group of about forty to fifty residents gathered along the shore. Then they launched a snowmobile attack on the intruders and fired high-powered rifles. One observer reported that the bullets hit the UFOs like slugs hitting a garbage pail. Eventually the strange craft moved slowly out of the area.

As spring approached, these objects left deep impressions in the snow; some were seen hiding under trees in the bush; one was even seen going straight into the ground and disappearing. By summer, most of the activity ceased and only occasional sightings of the objects were made. Over the next few winters some UFOs put in an appearance on the lake, but the activity never reached the record set during the 1973 UFO flap.

During the summer of 1974 and on into the spring of 1975, reports of strange objects seen in the Lake Ontario region reached new heights. Some observers stated that the objects had a definite shape unlike conventional aircraft; others reported that they saw only lights that glowed brightly. In many cases the objects gave the impression that they were under intelligent control; others appeared to move randomly without apparent purpose.

Around 9 P.M. on March 13, 1975, a woman (name withheld for privacy), who was driving along the shore of Lake Ontario at Niagara-on-the-Lake, caught a glimpse of a cluster of lights near the shore. At first she assumed they were lights on a sand dredge operating on the lake, but as she passed by an opening in the trees she looked again and saw that they had moved. She went around the block and stopped to get a better look and saw that the lights were too bright for a barge. The lights were arranged in a triangular pattern of red and blue with the largest light, a silver color, at the bottom close to the water. Off to one side was another set of lights, which were gold-colored, and above these were two more lights that appeared to rise and fall.

The brightest of all the lights seemed to sway back and forth and was at least four times larger than any of the others. At times this light would vanish momentarily, then reappear.

Unable to figure out what the lights were, the woman went home and phoned her daughter, who also lived near the lake shore. The daughter said that she, too, had been watching the strange antics of the lights and added that, during the time when the lights had been near her home, the family dog had cowered in fear.

This sighting was confirmed by local police, who also viewed the lights while on patrol along the shore. However, there was no explanation as to what the lights were.

Mrs. D. Wilmot, a Burlington, Ontario, woman, looked out of her fourth-floor apartment window around ten forty-five on the evening of March 17, 1975, and thought she was seeing a flaming plane about to crash into Lake Ontario. She soon realized that this was no plane on fire.

It was, she said, a twenty-foot-long fluorescent object five feet high with a domed top that glowed orange. For five minutes she watched it from her window as it hovered fifteen hundred feet out from shore. It then appeared to oscillate and rise slowly upward and finally shot off to the west and was lost from view behind the corner of the apartment building.

None of the other residents of the building reported seeing anything unusual, but most admitted to having their drapes closed at that time.

The following day, the eighteenth, the Hamilton *Spectator* published a front-page photograph of a disk-shaped craft, or

UFO, that had been photographed a short distance outside Hamilton by a Waterdown High School student, Pat McCarthy. The student had been in the process of photographing wildlife in a nearby quarry when he looked up and saw the object. He had just enough time to photograph it, then it was gone.

Over the next few days, experts examined the photograph for evidence of a hoax but were unable to prove that the photograph had been rigged or tampered with in any way.

On the twentieth, a few days after this incident, another UFO sighting was made at Toronto's east end Beaches district. The objects were seen by two adults and several children from a pier on the beach at around 11:30 P.M. They were described as golden-colored and were seen traveling west down the lake and over the shore. At the time of the sighting the moon was visible, and one of the objects approached the observers and hovered for a short period before moving on. The witnesses described this one as appearing to be the size of the moon and exhibiting red and green lights. This one also shot off to the west at high speed.

During this sighting an aircraft passed by, allowing the observers to make a comparison of its lights to those of the UFO. But the hovering and the sudden high-speed maneuvers made the witnesses certain they were not observing any conventional aircraft.

Twice during the following week phantom lights put in an appearance. These were made during the evening hours close to the atomic power plant at Pickering on the shore of Lake Ontario between Toronto and Oshawa. In one of the sightings residents in the area observed the lights as they hovered near the shore and as they passed over the generating plant.

More than a dozen UFOs were counted passing overhead or maneuvering out over the lake.

The next sighting occurred around six-thirty one evening and lasted until eleven forty-five. At this time the lights were observed by five ambulance drivers, a police officer, and two radio newsmen. Before it was over, it had lasted six hours. In this sighting they were described as multicolored pulsating lights—blue, yellow, red, and green—but it could not be determined if they were attached to any sort of craft. When they were examined through binoculars, it was obvious they were not stars. The sightings were made from a point one and a half miles back from the shore and just east of Ajax, Ontario. At times the lights appeared to be just above the lake and moving to the west at a very slow pace.

Shortly after midnight one of the ambulance drivers observed another UFO. This one came in from the lake and passed over the 401 Highway and landed in a field a few hundred yards north of the westbound lane. When the ambulance driver and a UFO investigator visited the site the following morning, they discovered a burn ring in the field measuring almost thirty feet across. Strangely, none of the drivers on this busy section of highway seemed to have noticed the UFO and no other witnesses reported it.

By April 5, the strange lights were being observed just east of Oshawa. This time, Paul Smith, a salesman, sighted a cluster of colored lights as they traveled down the lake to the west. They were moving too rapidly for the man to get his binoculars to get a better view of them, but the sighting stirred his curiosity so much that he kept a close watch on the lake for the next few nights to see if the lights would make a return visit. On the eleventh, his vigilance paid off when he sighted a small cluster of lights a half mile above Oshawa. Within minutes after he called the police and the local newspaper editor, a police officer and the editor arrived at his home and together they watched the phenomenon for over an hour.

In the meantime, scanty newspaper reports showed that the lights were back in the southwest corner of Lake Ontario again. The reports aroused a young photographer and on the evening of April 8, Peter Werner set up his camera on the shore at Niagara-on-the-Lake and took a photograph on a five- to six-minute exposure of the lights as they performed over the water. The photograph shows several unusual lights streaking back and forth in independent maneuvers. In this photograph nearby tree branches and the skyline of Toronto, along with the eighteen-hundred-foot tall CN Tower on the opposite side of the lake, were clearly outlined and unblurred.

The photograph was made between 9 and 10 P.M. and a local UFO investigator, who called Toronto International Airport, learned that there were no commercial aircraft in that corner of the lake during that time. Even if there had been, the streaks in this photograph indicate abrupt halts and sharp turns that no aircraft built today could make.

Around 9:30 P.M. on the night of April 9, the wife of an aeronautical engineer sighted a group of strange lights out over the lake and called her husband, Harry B. Picken. This couple live near the shore of Lake Ontario where the Niagara River enters the lake, and from this vantage point they have a good view over the water. The husband ran out to the driveway, and with a pair of binoculars was able to get a clear look at the lights, which he later described as three yellow-orange globes arranged in triangular fashion. He estimated their height to be close to forty or fifty thousand feet. He stated that periodically the lights grew extremely bright and during this "blooming" they appeared much larger, then faded to almost nothing and began to grow bright again. This process was repeated time and again during the half hour that the couple observed the lights.

Picken further stated that when viewed through binoculars, each of the lights could be seen to be made up of two lights closely spaced on a horizontal plane with a slight space between them. However, at the times they faded out, they were replaced by numerous small flickering lights of various colors arranged in a haphazard fashion.

During the time of the sighting, all of the objects remained in the same position. In the end they simply faded away and did not return.

As this highly qualified aeronautical engineer pointed out late in 1977, he and his friends have often watched these pulsating orange lights over the lake. He is also aware that the area where the lights are most often seen is directly under the Vector 36 flight path into Toronto's International Airport. This, he said, allows a comparison with conventional aircraft lights. Unlike them, however, these lights are closer to that produced by sodium vapor and they appear to expend thousands of watts of energy when they are brilliant.

By July 6 the strange activity around Lake Ontario began to take on some new elements. That was the day when a UFO landed on the tobacco farm of Joe Borda, outside London, west of the lake. When the Provincial Police arrived to investigate the damage to his crops, they also took a sample of a bluish-green substance and sent it to a laboratory in

Toronto for analysis. Borda waited for a reply but heard nothing, and he then turned to a local UFO group.

According to Tom Grey, the editor of *UFO Update*, who supplied a copy of the report that he and members of Northeastern UFO Organization completed after investigating the case, this farmer had seen a shiny dome-shaped object sitting in one of his fields and assumed it was a tank truck doing some spraying on his crops. Two days later he went down to the field on a routine check and discovered that all of the tobacco plants in a twenty-foot circle had been damaged and burned. The police examined the place for signs of vandalism but found no evidence of this. When the UFO investigators got the call, they arrived and photographed the damaged area and collected some of the burned plants and took soil samples. They also gathered samples of the bluish-green substance for analysis. Later, when the photographs were developed, it was found that the twenty-foot area of damaged plants had a bluish tint not present in the undisturbed part of the field nearby. When the bluish-green substance was tested it was found to contain sand and an oily silicon-based substance of unknown composition.

The UFO investigators learned that the farmer had not reported the damage to the police right away. He had postponed it to the following day and was surprised when a limousine with Arizona license plates arrived at his farm and drove directly to the damaged area without stopping to get permission. Upset at the intrusion, Mr. Borda followed the limousine and its three occupants to the site and found them gathering samples. When he asked what they were doing, he was told that they were gathering samples and that he was to return to his work, that it was none of his business. For some reason, which the farmer could not explain, he immediately complied with their order without argument.

According to the UFO investigators, this case left them with several unanswered questions. They were puzzled by the fact that Borda had not demanded identification from the three men or ordered them off his property until the police had been notified. But what puzzled them most was how the three strangers knew about this UFO event when Borda had not yet reported it to anyone, and why had they arrived at the farm in a limousine with Arizona license plates.

Had these three men driven all the way from Arizona just to gather these samples? If so, who informed them about the UFO landing and whom did they represent? The UFO investigators are still trying to find out.

Sometimes news of UFO events does get around. The lights seen by the Oshawa salesman, the policeman, and the editor were written up in the Oshawa *Times* and a Cornwall, Ontario, truck driver, Gordon Barrie, contacted the newspaper to tell them that one evening, two days after the Oshawa sighting, he had seen exactly the same type of object coming down in a quarry at Cornwall, two hundred miles to the east. The object had first been seen hovering over the Domtar plant where it remained for five minutes, then it rose up and headed toward Lake Ontario.

On April 17 the Cornwall radio station carried a report phoned in by two different couples who had observed similar UFOs with red, green, and white lights. These UFOs had appeared above Number 2 Highway and were last seen following the road west.

In these accounts there is a similarity in all the descriptions given by the witnesses in widely scattered areas, indicating a close relationship that cannot be denied. Some appear to be nothing more than lights without a definite source, and none seem to fit the category of aircraft lights. There is even some evidence that the lights may be the result of some sort of propulsion system that powers the UFOs and this causes a radiation or halation in the visible portion of the spectrum. This appears to be the case in those sightings where a brilliant glow appears on top of, or underneath, a UFO just as it starts to speed away from the scene.

Some UFO investigators are inclined to believe that all such sightings, whether lights or objects, are all directly related to craft from another planet or dimension.

An equal number of UFO investigators reject all nocturnal lights as providing too little actual hard evidence to be worth investigating or as being related to some other little-known phenomenon and not part of the UFO events. Some have gone so far as to say that these nocturnal lights, while they closely resemble some of the well-documented descriptions of UFOs, are in reality "poltergeists," intended to distract the attention of the public from the true UFO events.

While this argument continues pro and con, there is one UFO investigator who believes the increasing activity of these nocturnal lights at the western end of Lake Ontario suggests something more than poltergeists.

Malcolm Williams, an investigator with the Northeastern UFO Organization, feels that the high percentage of these sightings in this one area adds support to the theory put out by Ivan T. Sanderson in his book *Invisible Residents*. Sanderson suggests that the UFOs are piloted by visitors from another planet and their appearances near water indicate that these beings are using the water areas of earth as bases for their operations.

Williams has examined maps showing the depths of Lake Ontario at the western end where the lights have been seen, and believes he has located two deep depressions joined by a long narrow channel. This, he says, could reinforce Sanderson's theory.

For the present, no underwater explorations of the area are planned, and it appears that these strange lights are destined to remain a mystery for some time yet.

# 8 UFOs Are Everywhere

During the early history of the Great Lakes region, the bulk of the mysterious events that occurred there involved ships. No doubt a lack of knowledge of the ways of these inland waters made these happenings seem inexplicable. Today, our knowledge of violent and unexpected storms in these waters has explained a considerable number of present-day marine events, and the emphasis has shifted to things taking place more on the land and in the sky. It has not, however, brought a complete end to the unexplained events on water. Attention is simply focused elsewhere.

Another reason for this shift may be a result of the advances made in communications. This has allowed news of events such as UFO sightings to reach a wider segment of the public, making them more aware of the existence of these unexplained phenomena. This has also brought to light some of the more bizarre incidents taking place. In these, witnesses claim to have observed alien craft landing; some claim to have been aboard these craft; others say they have actually taken trips in these craft to visit distant planets.

If these witnesses seem to lack credibility, they have no less than the witnesses who told of huge vessels vanishing from the surface of the water, of vessels battered by violent and unnatural forces, or of aircraft that crash into invisible barriers in the sky or disappear in an instant.

As was shown in the last chapter, 1975 brought a considerable increase in the number of UFO sightings around Lake Ontario. This was also true for other areas around the world. According to UFO groups keeping records of these events, the sightings in that year peaked during October and resulted in an astounding number of documented cases.

Even small communities like Bracebridge, Ontario, eighty-five miles north of Lake Ontario, were drawn into the headlines. Here, on the evening of November 7, a young farmer named Robert Suffern received a phone call from a relative living a short distance away telling him there was a bright glow near one of his farm buildings. Thinking that it might be a fire, the young farmer rushed out and drove down the lane to where the buildings were located. But he found nothing wrong. Just to be sure, he drove out onto the road adjoining his property. Rounding a curve, he slammed on his brakes as his pickup almost hit a glowing, silver-suited humanoid creature standing in the middle of the road. While the farmer sat stunned, the glowing figure glided to a fence, floated over it, then vanished in the bush without appearing to touch the ground!

The farmer was astounded, to say the least. He was even more astounded when he turned back and saw what was sitting in the center of the road. It was a metallic, saucer-shaped craft and it had the gravel road blocked completely.

When the farmer regained his senses, he spun the pickup around and raced back up the road to the house and called the local detachment of the Provincial Police.

The call for help brought more than the farmer bargained for. When the police arrived they searched the area thoroughly and questioned him, but the net result was zero. No alien beings or craft were found, and the only evidence of anything unusual was the farmer's account of what had happened. Although the police may have believed his story, there was absolutely nothing they could do about the encounter. Instead, they turned their attention to something more tangible. News of the event had brought swarms of reporters and curious gawkers who plugged the narrow country roads and made a nuisance of themselves. Before the fervor had died down, the young farmer and his family were accused of seeking publicity and lying about the whole event. Nothing could have been further from the truth.

In the weeks following the incident, sightseers were still roaming the back roads around the small community in daylight and darkness in search of the mysterious beings and their strange craft. None was ever sighted.

While the sightseers around Bracebridge were having no success, that was not the case with residents two hundred miles to the southwest. At Madison, Ohio, strange lights were reported coming in from Lake Erie. At 3:30 A.M. on November 4, a group of residents phoned local police to report seeing more of them. Two patrolmen, Zachary Space and Lester Nagle, were sent to investigate and they arrived in time to see two clusters of lights in the sky separate. One cluster streaked toward the town of Madison while the other continued to hover in an area near power lines.

For a time the patrolmen and the residents stood watching the cluster as it moved closer to the power lines, and then Patrolman Nagle decided to shine the car's spotlight on the cluster to see if they could get a better look at what the strange thing actually was. But the light beam seemed to drive the object farther away. Then for some reason the patrolman decided to flick the light off and on a few times. This seemed to attract the object and it came closer to the ground and started to come toward the observers. Almost immediately the patrolman decided that this wasn't such a good idea and he snapped the light off. The object then returned to the higher altitude and the power lines a half mile distant.

According to the description given by witnesses, the object was huge but difficult to see in the dark. Most of the time all that could be seen were the green and white lights, which appeared to be on the bottom of the object, and a red light, which was much larger and on top. At times these lights were lost from view as the whole object became a brilliant white. This happened each time the object was very close to the power lines.

One of the observers estimated the size of the object by holding up his hand at arm's length so as to cover the object while it hovered near the lines. Even then the object was larger than his hand.

For the next hour and a half the group watched as this strange object slowly maneuvered close to the power lines and, although it was never seen to touch the lines, turned white. At this point the object would then zoom off so fast that none of the observers could follow it. When the bril-

THE LOSS OF THE SPEEDY

In 1804 an Indian, Ogetonicut, arrested near York, was accused of murdering a trader, John Sharp, at Lake Scugog. The trial was to be held here in the projected, but never completed, district town of the Newcastle District. On October 7, the schooner Speedy sailed from York. Her passengers, in addition to the prisoner, included Solicitor-General Robert Gray, Judge Thomas Cochrane, High Constable John Fisk and other participants in the trial. The ship appeared briefly off Presqu'ile on the 8th before vanishing forever. The loss of so many prominent persons was a severe blow to the small colony.

Erected by the Ontario Archaeological and Historic Sites Board.

7. & 8. The historic marker at Presqu'ile Park, above, commemorates the loss of the *Speedy* and all her crew and passengers. This gravestone, below, found in an isolated bush on the Covell farm at Brighton, marks the final resting place of Captain James Richardson, one of the *Speedy*'s two masters. His premonition of disaster failed to save the ship when authorities ignored his warnings. (Hugh Cochrane photos)

9. & 10. During storms on the lake, weather-wise sailors sought the protection of calm bays or coves like the one shown above. According to old-timers, this sheltered cove was often white with sails when the waters rose in fury. Below, a graveyard in Prince Edward County for sailors whose bodies washed up on shore. (Hugh Cochrane photos)

11. & 12. These two photographs show a nocturnal light over the shore of Lake Ontario. While the Toronto resident was taking the pictures outside his home, the object sped off at high speed without making a sound. Computer analysis revealed that the light came from an intense source capable of moving at extremely high speed. (Cliff Crocker photos)

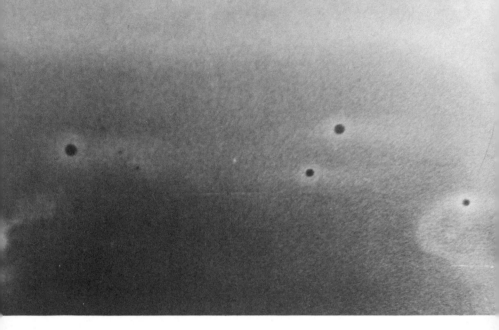

13. & 14. Numerous "light absorbing" UFOs have turned up in photographs in the past few years. No explanation has been found for them. The ones above were photographed over the western end of Lake Ontario. (Malcolm Williams photo) The time exposure below shows "nocturnal light" activity over the water, with the Toronto skyline and the 1,800-foot CN Tower in the background. (Harry Picken photo)

liance died away, it then changed back to red, white, and green and then returned to the power lines to resume the strange procedure. According to the observers, it appeared as if the object was using the power lines to recharge itself. All told, twenty such passes were made at the lines.

During this sighting neither the police nor tow truck's radios would operate. The police dispatcher in Madison had watched some of the events from a window. He had only ventured outside once, had seen the object hovering over the town, and had returned to his post at the radio.

Finally the two objects vanished and were not seen in the area again.

Most of the events at Madison were reported across the country, then little was heard of the matter again. What was not revealed was that several of the witnesses received visits from men who claimed to be U. S. Government representatives. What seemed rather odd about this was that these representatives appeared to show very little interest in the actual events that had taken place. They seemed more interested in making it clear that the witnesses were to say nothing more about the incident, nor to mention that they had been told to remain silent, and particularly they were to say nothing about what had occurred *under* the power lines!

In a personal communication with one of these witnesses, I was informed that "there hadn't been much damage [under the power lines] and as long as no one got hurt the locals wouldn't start anything." However, he would not say what it was that had happened under the power lines.

Interest in the Madison event died quickly when the wire services reported that a Herber, Arizona, logger named Travis Walton had been "abducted" by a UFO. Like the Bracebridge farmer's story, newspaper readers tended to class this event as nothing but a hoax. While a thorough search was made to find this logger, his companions, who said they had seen him being abducted, were given lie detector tests. In the end the authorities were left baffled and it appeared that Walton was on his way to another planet.

On November 10, the crew aboard the *Edmond Fitzgerald* had more to do than wonder about strange lights or UFO abductions. Earlier in the week the ship had taken on twenty-six thousand tons of pelletized iron ore at Superior, Wisconsin, for the blast furnaces at Detroit. Since then they had traveled over three hundred miles of Lake Superior's dark waters and were now being lashed by a storm with a fury that few had ever witnessed.

By 7 P.M. the *Fitzgerald* appeared to be having difficulty. She had taken on water from the heavy seas and her captain, Ernest R. McSorley, was becoming concerned. At 7:10 P.M. he radioed another ship, the *Arthur Anderson*, a few miles behind and requested that they keep the *Fitzgerald* on their radar. He gave no indication that his ship was in any immediate danger, and from time to time the crew of the *Anderson* had visual contact with the other ship. Minutes later, however, the crew of the *Anderson* lost both visual and radar contact with the *Fitzgerald*. It had vanished completely from the surface of the lake. Like the *Picton* in 1900, one minute she was there and the next she was gone.

A call was immediately sent to the United States Coast Guard, and other vessels in the area were alerted to be on the lookout for any survivors of the *Fitzgerald*'s twenty-nine-man crew. Within a few hours five ships and three aircraft were scouring the immediate area where the huge freighter had last been seen and the search spread out from there. But no trace of the $8 million vessel or her crew turned up. In this area of Lake Superior the bottom drops to a record thirteen hundred feet. At that depth the water is black and cold, and the light of day never penetrates. It was into this chasm that most searchers believed the *Fitzgerald* had gone. But the uppermost question was how she had vanished so fast.

It was almost three years after the event before answers began to trickle in. First was that the remains of the 729-foot vessel had been found in 530 feet of water on August 1, 1977. The huge freighter had been knifed in two with her bow half and stern half lying close to each other. At a hearing before the U. S. National Transportation Safety Board, some argued that the ill-fated vessel had hit an uncharted shoal, while others expressed the belief that there had been a sudden massive flooding of the cargo hold, which resulted from the collapse of a hatch cover. By May 1978, it was ruled that the hatch covers had been damaged and this was the prime cause of the disaster.

Nonetheless, members of the Lake Carriers Association felt that there was evidence the ship had hit uncharted shoals that had been discovered by divers during the underwater investigations. However, no one seems to know why these shoals were never discovered before or why none of the vessels that had sailed into that same area on November 11, 1975, had struck any shoals.

The investigations into the sudden sinking of this vessel brought to light a different explanation. It was offered to the government investigators by Lyle McDonald of Laurium, Michigan, a long-time commercial fisherman on Lake Superior who has the support of many old Great Lakes sailors. He proposed that the *Fitzgerald* had been hit by the "three sisters," a trio of killer waves often known to sweep across these waters. Old shipping records mention these strange waves, and even Indian legends in this area tell of them, saying that the waves are spawned deep in the lake. But the case has been closed and no other solutions are required.

When the facts were all in, it became apparent that not all of the fury of the November 10 storm had been spent on Lake Superior. It had also slammed into Lake Erie, and local police reported that waves from that lake had swept into homes along the north shore. At one point the water levels shot up fifteen feet, and a search was made for missing Lake Erie fishermen. From all of this, one thing was certain: This storm would find its way into the history of the Great Lakes. At the time of writing, a film, *The November Gale*, is in production to commemorate this dramatic event.

While newspaper readers around the Great Lakes followed these developments, readers in Arizona got details on something quite different. On November 11, papers there announced that Travis Walton had returned from his trip to another planet. He had regained consciousness and found himself lying on a highway outside Herber, Arizona, where he had been left by the UFO that had returned him to earth.

On November 11, Great Lakes area newspapers got their own UFO stories when strange lights appeared in the sky over Sudbury, Ontario, two hundred miles east of the point where the *Fitzgerald* had gone missing. The articles told how the switchboards at the NORAD center there had been flooded by calls reporting UFOs in the sky, while at Falkenbridge, twelve miles to the east, the NORAD radar screens were alive with unknown objects. As operators at the center tried to process these calls, more came in from Haileybury, ninety miles to the northeast. Whatever they were, they seemed to be turning up all over the area.

Almost immediately, the data systems at NORAD head-quarters at Colorado Springs began receiving the information on the sightings. An alert was flashed to the Selfridge Air Force Base north of Detroit and within minutes jet fighters were airborne and streaking north toward Sudbury. Mean-while the UFOs continued to maneuver in and out of the light cloud cover hanging over the northlands. When the fighters arrived on the scene and began to zero in on their tar-gets, the UFOs zoomed up to higher altitudes and were lost from sight.

As the speeding jets passed over Falkenbridge they made a wide sweep without picking up anything on their radar. They continued in a wide arc that took them close to the area of Lake Superior where the search was going on for the missing ore freighter.

The jets were unable to locate anything and the UFOs were no longer on the NORAD screens. Colorado Springs or-dered the jets to return to their base and the search for the UFOs came to an end.

But the excitement had only shifted. At Niagara Falls, On-tario, attendants at a large game farm became concerned when the animals started acting strangely. Something was def-initely wrong. Particularly with the fifteen-hundred-pound buffaloes. While the attendants struggled to calm the other animals, the huge buffaloes battered their way out of their heavy steel-mesh enclosures and five of them escaped before they could be stopped. Police were called in to help recapture the animals. After hours of searching, four of the buffaloes were caught and returned to their pens. The fifth had to be shot when it charged down a superhighway, threatening to cause traffic accidents.

Was this upset among the animals due to unexplained

forces generated by the storm? Was it something similar to the "Voice of the Sea" or ultrasonic sounds like those proposed by the Russian scientists? An aftermath of the fury of the storm that had swept the Great Lakes?

In the early hours of November 12, the UFOs returned to the skies over the northlands. This time the reports were passed down the line, then filed away. Apparently authorities decided that nothing could or would be done about these mysterious objects and simply returned to their "business as usual" routine.

However, news-hungry papers were not without a good story. When the freighter *Arthur Anderson* docked at Sault Ste. Marie, Michigan, the press was on hand to interview her captain. He had been the last person to communicate with the *Fitzgerald* seconds before it had vanished. But the experience had drained him and when he came ashore he brushed the reporters aside and refused to comment.

By the middle of the week a flurry of speculation arose when it was reported on the twelfth that an empty dinghy had been found on Lake Superior by one of the search parties. There was no identification on the dinghy, but a knife was found to be missing from one of its survival pouches. All of this was offered as a brief mention, leaving readers to speculate on the possibility that survivors might have encountered some sort of menace and were forced to fight for their lives. But in the end most agreed that the huge ore carrier had vanished too suddenly to allow anyone to escape.

Through the rest of November, the UFOs made intermittent appearances around the Great Lakes region. When things quieted down, those interested in UFO events switched their attention back to the Travis Walton case. But not for long. Toward the end of 1975, residents near Madoc, Ontario, just forty-five miles north of Lake Ontario, began sighting UFOs.

The pattern was the same as in other cases. While some observers saw nothing more than a cluster of lights hovering and moving about at treetop height, others saw metallic disk-shaped craft that appeared to be under intelligent control.

At a small settlement called Cooper, a few miles north of Madoc, a resident was attracted by a disk-shaped UFO that hovered above a highway while red, green, and white lights pulsed around the rim of the craft. This sighting lasted for twenty minutes, and at one point the craft came down in a field less than a quarter of a mile from the home of the woman observing it. She watched it closely for a few minutes before it took off, making a high-pitched humming sound.

By the beginning of 1976, UFO reports were coming from the area near the eastern end of Lake Ontario and the St. Lawrence River. In one case a woman driving along a highway near Napanee caught sight of a triangular arrangement of lights, which swept down from a high altitude to treetop level and then began to follow her car down the highway. At one point she slowed down to get a better look at the object and became frightened when it came close to her car. When another car approached from the opposite direction the UFO quickly moved up and away from the highway. This gave the woman an opportunity to flee the area.

The woman sensed that whatever the object was, it was not the sort of thing she wanted to get involved with. Others have expressed a similar fear, which has gripped them during these encounters. But for some, this knowledge has come too late.

An example of this strong sense of danger that came too late is the case of Patrolman George Wheeler. In April 1976, he encountered a UFO at close range while on police patrol in Pierce County, Wisconsin. When the encounter was over, he was never the same again.

Late in the evening of April 22, 1976, Wheeler was patrolling a back road. He topped a rise known locally as Tuttle Hill and was on his way down the other side when he saw a huge craft hovering a hundred feet above the road. He estimated the object to be about two hundred and fifty feet in diameter with an orange-white light on top and six bluishwhite lights arranged around the rim.

Pulling to a stop a hundred and fifty yards from the object, Wheeler got out of his patrol car to get a better view. According to his observations there was a hatch or panel on the underside of the craft and it was open. Through it Wheeler could see what appeared to be a large finned rotor in the center of the craft and this was turning at a very slow rate. Now and then he caught a glimpse of small manlike figures moving about inside as if tending to this machinery.

On the bottom of the craft were legs like a landing gear and also a long black tube, which hung down to the ground beneath the hovering craft.

This strange sight stunned the patrolman but not as much as the sight of similar figures moving about on the ground under the craft. But he did not have time to see what they were doing, for they caught sight of him observing them and immediately boarded the huge craft that shot up into the sky.

Evidently Wheeler had been close enough to this UFO to become affected by some sort of radiation given off by the craft or its propulsion system when it took off, because at that point he collapsed to the ground. He was found later by a passing motorist who rushed him to a nearby hospital.

For the next few days Wheeler suffered from amnesia and

other undefined ailments as a result of the encounter. The doctors were puzzled by his condition. During the two weeks he spent in the hospital, they were unable to diagnose his ailments and he was released.

When Wheeler regained his memory and recounted the incident with the UFO, his story was refuted by skeptics. For the next few months, Wheeler tried to convince others of the hazards posed by radiation given off by UFOs. But his warnings went unheeded. For eleven months after the encounter he was unable to resume his duties with the police department.

In a communication from Mrs. Wheeler in 1977 I was informed that her husband had died. In the opinion of UFO investigators and writers who have studied the physical effects resulting from encounters with certain types of UFOs, Wheeler's death was a direct result of some sort of radiation given off by the UFO he encountered on that country road.

Two days after Patrolman Wheeler was taken to the hospital, observers around the western end of Lake Ontario reported to newspapers that the strange lights had returned— the same orange and white lights with some showing red and green in a cluster. They pulsated, moved up and down, and were seen entering and leaving the water.

By June 12, around 10:30 P.M., the lights were being reported halfway down the lake at Colborne on the north shore. For forty-five minutes, a couple living there watched the antics of a brilliant white light, with red and green on either side, as it zigzagged close to the lake at treetop height. At times it moved behind trees and was lost from sight, then it would reappear again.

During the time the object was in the area, the husband

and wife tried repeatedly to phone the police and relatives to alert them to the phenomenon. But their phone was mysteriously dead and remained so until the light left the area.

On May 12, 1976, the small community of Cooper, north of Madoc, Ontario, got another visit from a UFO. This time it left behind indisputable proof that there is more to these strange objects in the sky than can be passed off as being imagination or mirages.

Just north of this small community Reginald Trotter, a farmer, went into one of his fields and discovered three very large holes that should not have been there. There were no tracks of any sort leading in or out of the field, no sign that any machinery had been brought in to do the job. Still three five-hundred- to eight-hundred-pound chunks had been removed from the ground *intact* and dumped undisturbed almost fifty feet from where they had been excavated!

Trotter could not understand how it had happened and called the local police. But instead of finding an answer, the police left the farm as baffled as the farmer. They advised him to get in touch with the government to see if someone there could solve the mystery. However, this proved to be a futile effort. Thinking that the holes might have something to do with the UFOs seen in the area, Trotter got in touch with the Air Force, which in turn passed him on to an "expert." This "expert" then informed him that the chunks of earth were probably blasted out of the ground by lightning bolts. But there had been no storms in the district during the time when Trotter estimated the chunks had been removed, which was some time during the previous two weeks. Furthermore, people in the area, who were familiar with the effects of lightning strikes on soil, all stated that lightning always leaves furrows. This claim was supported by a high-voltage engineer who was later questioned on the matter.

When Trotter tried to press the matter further, he was referred to the Defence Department, which referred him to the Provincial Police Headquarters, which referred him to the local detachment, which had originally referred him to the government. In short, it would appear that Trotter had been "stonewalled."

I spoke with several of the investigators from Reptune Research, a Toronto-based UFO group, who had learned of the mystery and had gone to the site to conduct an investigation. The holes on Trotter's farm were found to be inside the northeast half of a roughly circular area twenty feet in diameter. Photographs were taken, a sketch was made of the holes, and samples of the soil were gathered for analysis. However, none of this provided a solution to the mystery.

In an effort to determine what type of machinery could remove such large chunks of soil intact, the researchers contacted a construction machinery manufacturer. He assured them that there was no such machinery available that could do the job. Nor was there anything available that would not leave some sort of claw marks in the holes or on the chunks of sod.

One thing the researchers *did* uncover when they questioned other residents in the area was that there had been numerous unreported sightings of UFOs in and around the Cooper area since 1975, and among these were suspected landings.

In one case, which occurred on December 11, 1975, a local woman, Mrs. Pauline Dudgeon, had gone out to check on a brilliant glow, which was coming from the road in front of her home. When she reached the road she found that the glow was coming from a metallic saucer-shaped craft that had landed in the middle of the road. On its top was a red dome and around the outer edge were bright revolving lights.

This woman never went any closer than three hundred yards to the object but was so puzzled and attracted by it that she stood watching it for about twenty minutes. When she finally turned away to go into the house, the bright glow persisted in her vision and impaired her eyesight. This condition lasted for several days and she required treatment by an eye specialist, who suggested that her condition was similar to that of a person who had watched a welder's arc.

Like many other such cases, this one was never reported and therefore never fully investigated because the family feared ridicule.

There were other sightings during this December period. In one of these the UFO observed was described as oval-shaped, with four beams of light projecting from the bottom. In following up some of these accounts, Toronto UFO researchers came across an isolated field in which they found approximately two hundred rings, each eighteen inches in diameter, and five rings that measured thirty to forty feet across.

These researchers concluded that this area of Madoc had experienced a considerable number of UFO events, most of which had either gone unnoticed or unreported. They also theorized that the holes left on Reginald Trotter's farm were positive evidence that the UFOs had used some sort of antigravity mechanism, and this had caused the chunks of sod to be removed from the earth and deposited intact some distance away. In their estimation, the eye damage suffered by the woman was proof that the UFOs were more than imagination and certainly more than a mirage.

During the summer of 1976, the bulk of the reports of UFO sightings were duplicates of earlier ones. Most of the local UFO groups did not have the resources to thoroughly investigate each one of them, and the majority were put on file. Local newspapers in the areas that had previously covered UFO events gave their columns over to other matters.

Among the few that did make it into print was one that took place at 3 A.M. around the beginning of September. The location was the small community of Little Britain near the shore of Lake Scugog, north of Lake Ontario. Here a resident awoke and glanced out the window and thought he was seeing the moon reflecting off the waters of the lake. But when he glanced up in the sky, he saw a bright circular object with red and white lights rotating around its rim.

He decided that he was seeing a star in the process of breaking up and called his wife and their thirteen-year-old son. After watching it for a quarter of an hour, they decided that the object was not a star. It appeared to be too close, too mechanical in its rotation, and it had remained at the one location.

Almost twenty-five minutes after the man had first sighted the object, it began to move slowly to the southwest—in the direction of Toronto—and finally vanished.

Over the next few weeks similar sightings occurred in this area. Some lasted a few minutes, others up to half an hour. In all of these cases the objects were last seen moving southwest toward Toronto and the western end of Lake Ontario.

During this same period, a thirty-foot ring of burned and

swirled swamp grass was discovered on Washburn Island in Lake Scugog. A resident of the area who works with CUFORN (Canadian UFO Research Network), a Toronto UFO group, examined the site and discovered three evenly spaced indentations in the ground inside the circle. There were no tracks of any sort leading in or out of the area where the circle was found.

Burned rings at alleged UFO landing sites have caused many arguments. Some authorities, such as those at the Herzberg Institute of Astrophysics in Ottawa, Canada, state that these "burnt rings in the grass are well known to agricultural scientists and golf course operators throughout the country. Circular rings of burnt grass are produced at certain times of the year by the action of the fairy-ring mushroom." However, according to those agricultural scientists, particularly those at the Biosystematics Research Institute of the Canadian Agriculture Department, the most common of the fairy-ring mushrooms is the *Marasmius oreades* species. They cannot grow up or down to any extent but continue their radial growth pattern along the surface. The central portion dies, leaving an expanding, living ring-shaped mycelium. These rings may be centuries old in undisturbed sites or only a few years old on new lawns.

None of this seems to apply to the numerous cases around the world where swirled grass and crops have been found to be burned or scorched ten or more inches up their stalks. Also, there are many documented cases where laboratory examination of samples of such burned vegetation revealed that the plants had been subjected to intense heat or strong radiation which turned the cells of the plants to a carbonlike substance.

The argument could be carried further to point out that quite often thirty-foot rings have been found where none had existed the day before, that the burn traces show on the surface of rocks found within the burn ring, and that the burns are also found on newly fallen branches that fell to the ground shortly before the occurrence of the burn ring.

All of this information was available to those who put forth the fairy-ring mushroom theory, and this reflects the depth of the analysis of the UFO phenomena by scientific bodies acting for governments. The same lack of proper analysis of the facts is obvious in the answers given to residents of the Scugog area who were told they probably had mistaken Venus or Mars for a UFO. There are simply no records to show that either of these planets had ever made a half-hour excursion that took it completely across the sky.

While the residents around Lake Scugog tried to puzzle out their dilemma, the UFOs moved farther south. In late September a bright object, estimated to be forty feet across, was observed landing in a cornfield near Grand Bend in southwestern Ontario. It flattened and swirled the crop in an area over seventy-five feet wide and left four indentations in the ground to mark the spots where something like landing gear had pressed into the earth.

A few days after that event the residents around Lindsay, in the Lake Scugog area, were again calling their local paper to report that the UFOs had returned. In typical fashion they flashed red, green, and white lights while they hovered, then headed southwest.

At 12:30 A.M. on January 8, 1977, a woman living near Napanee, at the eastern end of Lake Ontario, phoned the police to report that a forty-foot disk-shaped object making a droning sound was hovering over her property at treetop height. The object appeared to be tipped at an angle as it rotated counterclockwise while three bright yellow-colored lights glowed around the rim and illuminated her backyard. While she was still talking to the police on the phone, the UFO rose to a higher altitude and the lights changed from yellow to blue. When the police arrived at her home they were able to observe the object for a few minutes before it sped away.

On January 15, 1977, the police in Bath, Ontario, at the eastern end of the lake, were called to watch a UFO. When they arrived at the scene they watched as it hovered for forty-five minutes over the Lennox Generating Station. During this time it swooped down over the village, changing from red to blue. Finally it streaked upward and disappeared from view.

During the summer of 1977, four UFOs put on a demonstration over London, Ontario, west of the lake. While they maneuvered above the airport, the local police and radio stations logged over seven hundred phone calls from witnesses observing the sight. A private pilot, who spotted them while approaching the airport, went up from four thousand feet for a closer look. He got close to one of the objects and described it as cylindrical in shape. When he angled his plane to shine his landing lights on it, the lights burned out.

In this sighting the objects, which were said to be a red color, had formed into a rectangle for five minutes, then formed a triangle when one left. In the end they all headed toward the northeast.

What may have been the strangest UFO report was one phoned in to the police in Middleport, New York, by a woman who described the object as boxcar-shaped, forty feet long, and ten feet high. It had hovered close to her home at treetop height while it released two silvery objects, which sped off to the south while the larger object slowly moved eastward and was lost from view.

On October 12, 1977, a single UFO appeared in the sky above Ogdensburg, New York, on the St. Lawrence River. This object was described as circular in shape, emitting a white and reddish glow. For a period of four hours this UFO made repeated appearances, maneuvered and changed color while residents watched. It departed for good after puzzling the observers with its strange activity.

This was the same general area where, in February 1915, the strange airplanes put in several appearances and confounded the residents. There was no solution for the phenomenon then, and a half century later there is still no solution.

# 9 Other Energies and Forces

Many events that occur in the Great Lakes region are classified as mysterious because they appear to defy natural laws. But do they? If a ship vanishes completely from sight or an aircraft has a wing sheared off in midair or humanlike creatures are seen with strange crafts, these things are said to be unnatural and impossible only because they do not fit within the framework of our scientific beliefs. But if, for instance, it was discovered that another dimension or an invisible world coexisted alongside our own, then a ship vanishing into it, or visitors arriving from it, would be no more unnatural than a voyage to Europe. The impossible would be a scientific fact and therefore no longer a mystery.

Allowing this, it could then be said that the amount of mysteriousness in these events is a measure of human knowledge. There may be a scientific explanation for all of these puzzling events, but the mechanism behind them has still not been discovered.

Seeking solutions to the worldwide mysteries seems to have become a fad since the 1950s. Among the Bermuda Triangle researchers and writers, there is a growing belief that the events in that area are due to radiations from the power source of the ancient Atlanteans. For the Russian scientists who probed that area of the ocean with their scientific equipment, the incidents could be due to ultrasonic sounds producing destructive vibrations. To many of the UFO believers, an outside intelligence and the excursions of alien beings are at the root of it all.

Strangest of all might be the theory proposed by a physicist whose spare time is given over to research in areas of the unexplained. He privately expressed the opinion to one writer that the strange activities occurring in the Bermuda Triangle are the result of unexplored electromagnetic forces that are coming from deep under the sea floor. He feels that these forces of raw energy swirl to the surface of the ocean and into the sky to create conditions that defy the laws of time and space. These forces are said to do this by "tunneling" through our perceived reality, creating temporary pathways into other dimensions that exist alongside our own reality, yet have remained unknown to us.

This tunneling, if it exists, might operate much like the methods used in electronics in which certain potentials, when applied to a crystal interface as in transistors, permit currents to tunnel through barriers between two circuits. Applied to the earth's crust (in which minerals are held together by a crystalline lattice, and which may be under high pressure or seismic stress), such tunneling might be brought about by energies generated deep in the mantle of the earth, thrusting through the rock and across faults or fissures to give birth to surges of strong electromagnetic radiation that escape to the surface. Such eruptions might be short-lived but potentially destructive.

In their experiments the two Dutch psychics, Gerard Croiset and Warner Tholen, are said to have detected erupting energies that were temporary and triggered only at certain times. As stated earlier, this triggering seemed to occur with the passage of the moon over the earth when its field interacted with the earth's field.

Applying this to the above theory of tunneling, the Dutch psychics may have been detecting those areas where energies generated in the earth are triggered into eruptions that reach up into the atmosphere. Like an unseen wind coming through an open door, the eruption ceases when the door is closed.

The concept of interdimensional worlds is one that has been used by science fiction writers for years. It is based on the proposition that a twin world, much like our own, could exist in the same space we occupy, yet be separated from us because of a difference in the phase of the fundamental frequency or vibration governing matter in both realities.

If true, both worlds could theoretically coexist and occupy the same space because both do not exist materially at the same time. They are separated by the phase difference in their matter.

This condition would be akin to two electric lamps pulsing on and off at exactly the same frequency, but 180 degrees out of phase. When one lamp is on, the other is off. If an observer were to blink at the same rate as one of the lamps, one lamp would appear to be continually on and the other off. If the lamps could be mounted one inside the other and each lamp visible only when lit, then an observer blinking as before would never be aware of the existence of the other lamp.

If another world or dimension exists that could be tunneled into by natural forces in this world, then it is equally possible that such a phenomenon could exist that would allow tunneling from the other world. If so, then it might be possible that the inhabitants of this other realm are also aware of this facility and are making use of it. In fact, this concept might provide the explanation needed to account for UFOs and their occupants, who have repeatedly been observed defying known laws of time and space and who appear and disappear instantly.

Along this line of reasoning is a statement made by a man in Monterey Bay, California, who claimed he was given a ride in a UFO on January 30, 1965. During the trip to some nearby mountains and back, he asked one of the humanoid creatures on the craft where they had come from. The reply was that they were from a planet which we do not see because it is hidden by a planet which we do see! Many UFO believers interpret this as evidence of interdimensional travel by the UFO entities.

Persinger and Lafrenière (in *Space-Time Transients*) suggest that such dimensional transfers would require an unknown mechanism the reverse of matter-energy conversion. At present we know that matter is exchanged for heat energy, as in burning wood, coal, or oil, but there is no understanding of any energy-to-matter process such as would be required to return an object to material form after passing into another dimension.

Whether the mechanisms are known or unknown, many of those who witnessed the *Picton* vanishing in 1900, or who saw Craig Carlisle's blip fade off the radar screens when his plane vanished in December 1977, could be convinced that Lake Ontario possesses a gateway to oblivion.

As yet there is no hard evidence to support any one theory. They are still just theories. But they point to some of the possibilities being seriously considered by UFO and triangle researchers and writers who are seeking a solution to the mysteries. In the meantime, evidence is accumulating from other sources that may bolster at least one of these theories.

As an example, in the book *Breakthrough to Creativity*, detailing some of her investigations into the special abilities of psychically gifted individuals, Dr. Shafica Karagulla reveals some of the astounding feats these people performed. She worked with people who could read closed books chosen at random, who could see inside the human body without the need of X rays, or who could probe the minds of other individuals whether nearby or at a distance.

One of these gifted subjects explained to Dr. Karagulla that on going to sleep at night she immediately found herself transported into university-like surroundings where she attended lectures on various subjects of her choice.

During one of these lectures—which she attended along with other students—she told how the instructor used "thoughtforms" as models to demonstrate various scientific principles. At one point, while the subject of the atom was being discussed, the instructor explained the neuron, which he called a "sound binder," and described its energy as being similar to narrow-band ultrasonic frequencies, yet vibrating at different rates for different elements.

More important was that during this lecture the instructor had interrupted the lesson and drawn attention to two Russian students who were present, telling them that the Russians had "lost" several good scientists when they had accidentally stumbled onto the frequency affecting the *iron* atom!

It is not known what became of the Russian scientists who inadvertently made the discovery. However, it is known that if the nucleus of the atom—the stabilizing mechanism—is disrupted, then the atom can disintegrate.

The human body contains small amounts of iron. So did the huge freighter *Edmond Fitzgerald* contain iron—twenty-six thousand tons of it. Also, the *Protostatis* carried a full load of scrap iron when it entered the Marysburgh Vortex. Both were caught in sudden furious storms and, if the theory offered by the Russian scientists concerning the "Voice of the Sea" is allowed, they may have been subjected to destructive ultrasonic sounds.

According to the findings of the government board investigating the sudden loss of the *Edmond Fitzgerald*, the ship sank because it filled with water. But at what point was the hull knifed in half? Was this in some way due to the "tuning" of the sound binder in the mass of iron aboard the vessel, brought about by ultrasonic sounds created by the storm?

If the information uncovered by Dr. Karagulla in the 1960s is any indication that the Russians were on the threshold of some startling discoveries, they certainly have not shared any of their findings with the rest of the world.

In recent years many experiments have been carried out in an attempt to learn more about ultrasonic waves. Whatever else was learned from these experiments, it is known that the investigations have led scientists to develop anticrowd and antitheft weapons for use against humans.

In an article in the *New Scientist*, March 29, 1973, it was revealed that Allen International, a major supplier of police and military equipment, had developed what they call a photic driver. The device makes combined use of strobe lights and loud noise, but the light is infrared and the sound ultrasonic. In use, almost nothing is seen or heard, yet the effects can be devastating to humans. The ultrasonic frequency most effective was found to be around 19.2 kHz, which induced nausea, giddiness, disorientation, and often severe headache. In some tests it was found that the sounds produced can persist in the human ear for hours afterward—a condition known as tinnitus—and can result in severe earache.

The strobe frequency used in the device is 15 Hz, the most critical flash rate as far as humans are concerned. This was the range said to be responsible for the flicker-fit phenomenon discovered by Dr. William Grey Walter and his associates in earlier experiments with strobe lights. At these rates epileptic fits have been induced in humans.

The photic driver was developed by Charles Bovill, chief engineer of the company, and it was mentioned that the use of infrared light—invisible to the human eye—allowed the light flashes to easily penetrate closed eyelids. This, combined with the ultrasonic waves capable of penetrating the human body without going through the ears, would incapacitate anyone at whom the device was directed.

While these developments do little to improve the moral standing of today's science, it does suggest that there may be links between the nausea, disorientation, and inability to function properly that is experienced by pilots and seamen in the Great Lakes region and ultrasonic or other forces being radiated in this area. It is also notable that people who have come in close contact with UFOs have often reported experiencing similar effects. Obviously Patrolman Wheeler suffered side effects from his encounter in April 1976, and he died within eleven months. Finally, another article on the use of ultrasonic intruder alarms in *New Scientist,* November 8, 1973, describes the physical problems experienced by people entering buildings where the devices are in use. These include those already mentioned plus fatigue and migraine headaches among employees and customers in buildings when the alarms were left on during the day. One installer even refused to have anything more to do with the devices.

Science has found many ways to use ultrasonic waves. Today they are used to clean clothes and jewelry by vibrating cleaning fluids into small cracks and crevices; other frequencies and levels are used to penetrate injured muscles where the vibrations generate localized areas of heat.

It is particularly interesting that high-frequency sounds can also create a fog or mist if conditions are damp or humid. This brings to mind those cases where, before an aircraft suddenly vanished or crashed for unexplained reasons, the pilots reported that they were in a fog or mist and could not see the horizon or tell up from down.

# 10 The Search for Answers

Of all the theories suggested as solutions to mysteries discussed in this book, those most likely to receive at least a hearing from the scientific community are the ones proposing undiscovered natural forces. This is because there is a possibility that existing scientific laws could accommodate such forces. Whether they are due to ultrasonic or electromagnetic forces, they appear to be linked to already known fields and currents that flow in the complex circuitry composing all of the material matter of this earth. These may also be under the influence of natural events, terrestrial and extraterrestrial, yet they seem as real and as invisible as the well-known global magnetism and its elastic lines of force permeating the globe and the space around it.

Further, these appear to be the same forces and energies well known to the leaders of ancient civilizations, who were able to derive benefits from these natural phenomena. In the ages since then, this knowledge appears to have been forgotten. Only fleeting mention of it is made in the folklore and

mythology handed down from generation to generation. But
even this has been misunderstood and misinterpreted in this
age of big science and materialism.

These naturally produced forces are now largely ignored ex-
cept when they erupt suddenly and confront mankind with
the undeniable fact that there still are unexplained realms
existing all around us. It is these that appear to be causing the
mysterious events in the triangles and zones of mystery
around the world.

If that sounds like an oversimplification, then be warned. It
is not. It is only the tip of the iceberg.

There are other energies known to science but not widely
accepted as important—energies that exist around all matter
living or nonliving. As an example, electrical fields are known
to exist around the human body and these have been measured by investigators like Dr. Harold S. Burr and Dr. Leonard
Ravitz, working at the Yale University School of Medicine.
They called it the L-field or the field of life. According to
their findings, this energy exists beyond the familiar electromagnetic spectrum. As they explain it, every living thing
on this planet, whether animal or vegetable, is molded and
controlled by electrodynamic fields, which can be measured
with any sensitive voltmeter. They demonstrated that these
fields reveal both the physical and mental abnormalities in
humans long before the conditions become manifest as actual
physical symptoms.

These fields appear to be quite similar to the auras psychics
have spoken of for centuries (see page 95). These radiations
surrounding the human body are said to be like fine lines of
light in pastel colors from blues to reds, and their strength
and depth of color are related to an individual's physical condition.

As mentioned earlier, mineral crystals are also said to possess similar glowing fields of energy. Here again, colors are present, and these along with the vortices and converging lines are different for every type of mineral.

These strange displays seem to carry over even when the mineral is cut and fashioned into gemstones. Ancient texts reveal strong beliefs that certain gems when cut and mounted as jewelry retained powers capable of curing ailments, protecting the wearer against evil, or increasing psychic abilities. With the breastplate of Aaron—itself containing twelve cut gems said to represent the character of each of the twelve tribes—were two special stones, the Urim and Thummim, which were said to be able to answer yes or no questions for the high priest. The description of this artifact is contained in the Bible as well as other sources. Edgar Cayce, possibly one of America's greatest psychics, gave many readings while in psychic trances in which he recommended that certain gems or minerals be worn because of their electromagnetic influences.

In some of the experiments conducted by Dr. Karagulla to learn more about the fields around minerals and crystals, she placed crystals close to a hi-fi while various types of music were played. According to the psychics observing the crystals, the fields responded to some types of music and became brighter or expanded their fields while fine lines of energy became sharper. Other types of music brought no response. But the psychics noted that when the response was greatest the effect would linger even after the music had been switched off.

It would seem that an understanding of these fields would be of great importance since the fields appear to exist even around the smallest grains of minerals. This knowledge might lead to a natural method of enhancing the power of certain minerals in the human body, thus triggering natural healing processes without having to resort to manufactured drugs.

If the findings of these scientists and psychics prove to have a basis in fact, then we might expect that our planet itself is alive with glowing fields and vortices, since it is composed of massive amounts of the same minerals and crystals. The whole world would be a veritable invisible forest of radiating energy.

Are these the energies being triggered by the passage of the moon to create the eruptions that the Dutch psychics felt were responsible for the mysteries of the Bermuda Triangle? There is no way of knowing for sure because the scientific establishment still does not fully accept psychics, much less their theories.

In the meantime there are other proposed sources of energy coming from the earth that the scientific community finds easier to accept. In their investigations into earthquake lightning, Drs. D. Finkelstein and J. Powell found that, in pre-fracture zones where seismic strain is increasing, the pressures exerted on the crystal structures in rock produce piezoelectric —voltage produced by distortion of crystals—effects. In some cases the electric fields reached potentials as high as thousands of volts per meter. They found that these fields can give rise to atmospheric ionization, which in turn can create luminous displays.

Dr. M. A. Persinger also found similar effects occurring in areas prior to earthquakes, and he suggested the possibility that infrasonic and ultrasonic waves might be generated by the increasing pressures. He further suggested the possibility that such electric energies, accumulating in local areas, could result in an electric column rising into the atmosphere. Even more interesting was the suggestion that these columns could affect living electrical systems and that the sensitivity demonstrated by animals before an earthquake might be due to these electrical energies, which the animals are detecting.

Is it possible that there is a connection between these columns of energy and the ones proposed by Wilbert Smith in the 1950s around Lake Ontario? The energies in the columns proposed by Persinger are said to be the result of *stresses* deep in the earth. The energies in the column proposed by Smith were most effective on those aircraft components that were under *stress*. Is high stress the key to the mystery of why the *Fitzgerald* was knifed in two? Certainly its twenty-six thousand tons of iron ore would have created enormous stresses in her hull each time a wave lifted her. If the final waves she encountered were the legendary "three sisters," then the stresses could have been unimaginable.

In Smith's theories the energies in the column acted on the nuclear binding forces to weaken them. When these forces encountered matter already under stress, their effects were such that the forces binding the matter together ceased to exist along the line of maximum stress and the material simply parted. In an aircraft in flight, the result was certain disaster.

A rather curious possibility concerning these columns was suggested by Persinger and Lafrenière in *Space-Time Transients*. They proposed that, under the right conditions, ionization of the air within the column could result in luminous anomalies, and that the rising energies could cause rocks or other dielectrics in the area to appear to pop out of the ground, rise into the air and, on falling, appear to be dropping from the sky.

These scientists are not alone in their speculations. Other scientists, particularly in Europe, have gone as far as suggesting that UFOs are actually plasmoids of glowing energy held aloft by invisible fields generated inside the earth. If the theory of the above two scientists is allowed, then the supporting invisible structures could be columns of energy created by stresses deep in the earth.

These two scientists also proposed that such columns could be mobile, their direction and movements determined by the deep-seated forces generating them. This mobility follows Wilbert Smith's findings. He found that the columns could move right out of the area. He also expressed the belief that the nuclear binding forces were stronger in the north and weaker in the south. If this can be taken to mean that the effects of the energies in the columns are greater in the south, then we might speculate that the effects would be equivalent to stronger energies in the column producing more dramatic events.

Nothing could be more dramatic in the south than the "rain" of rocks that fell on Chico, California, in 1923. On and off for a period of four months, rocks mysteriously fell out of the sky and pelted down on this small community causing increased alarm among the residents. Then the fall of rocks ceased and never occurred again. If this event was due to a mobile column raising rocks off the ground and carrying them through the sky and depositing them at another location, we might ask if it is not the same columns that rise in lakes and ponds and thus provide the weird rains of fish and frogs that have been recorded by Fortean investigators around the world. Such columns, generated by subsurface forces, could erupt anywhere, since the entire earth's surface, even under the oceans, is subject to seismic forces.

If there are energies in these columns that can levitate rocks from the surface of the earth, is it possible that they are the same forces that surface inside tombs and crypts to levitate caskets and burial artifacts and give rise to tales of haunted tombs? Have these same forces led archaeologists to believe that grave robbers had entered ancient tombs and scattered the artifacts, yet left the original seals on the entrance intact? These are just speculations, but if the columns are as energetic as these scientists propose, then the movement and levitation of other materials may not be too impossible.

Modern science recognizes three basic forces in the universe: electromagnetic, nuclear, and gravitational. While scientists do not question the relationship between nuclear forces and electromagnetism, the link between these and gravity has eluded understanding. Albert Einstein in his work on a unified field theory was concerned with this relationship, and after a lifetime of study the solution appeared to have defied all his efforts. The only one who seems to have come close to a sort of link between electricity and gravity is Townsend Brown, codeveloper of the Biefeld-Brown effect. His work in elastic stress in dielectrics has shown that if electrical potentials are slowly raised to high values, the result is an effect much like antigravity. In his experiments, Brown was said to be able to cause a small disk-shaped "air-foil" to fly in a circular path while giving off a bluish haze and emitting a hum. This description has similarities matching many reported UFOs.

The mysteries around the world abound in similarities. There are certain elements in each of them that suggest a common source behind the phenomena. This seems most obvious in the UFO phenomenon and, if suppositions are allowed, then it can be shown that the theories concerning columns or vortices of energy provide some interesting possibilities.

For example, if we permit that there are electromagnetic energies erupting from the earth in the columns or vortices, and that portions of these may become luminous due to ionization of the atmosphere, then it is possible that many of the UFOs are visual manifestations of this same phenomenon but at a very energetic stage. Evidence found at so-called UFO landing sites, such as the burned ring, swirled grass and crops, and the triangular pattern of three depressions, could support this proposal. The burned ring could be due to a high electrical discharge as the column or vortex collapses and the glowing portion touches the ground. The swirled grass or crops could result from a high electrical charge spinning within the column or vortex, electrostatically attracting vegetation in the direction of rotation. Since it was suggested that a rising column or vortex decreases gravity, then a collapsing column or vortex may increase gravity. Therefore, the three depressions could be due to a gravitational effect, the reverse of the effect that raises rocks into the air. In this way soil densities at the three depressions may be the result of increased gravity at these points where the concentration of energy entered the earth, rather than compaction due to the weight of an object.

Swirling energies rising up out of the earth? A visual glow or luminance? If we refer back to Father Lejeune's conversations with the shaman after the shaking tent ritual, he was told that the "spirits" were conical-shaped! During this ritual it was said that a force swirled around inside the tent and a multitude of pinpoints of light appeared above the apex of the tent.

This brings us to the question of just what sort of forces the shaman was invoking from the earth. Were they the same forces as those in the columns proposed by Smith, Persinger, and others? Are they all speaking about the same thing but addressing it differently?

There is one type of UFO-related phenomenon that is particularly suited to the energetic-column theory. This is one that has become prevalent over the past few years and has confounded UFO investigators and writers of the unexplained, to say nothing of the problems it has created for state authorities and farmers. This is the cattle mutilations that have plagued the midwestern United States since 1975. Since then, the carcasses of over nine thousand farm animals, mostly cattle, have been found mutilated in ways that defy description, others have just disappeared.

What is most puzzling about these cases is the way the cattle are mutilated. Genitals, udder, rectum, and tongues are the parts usually missing, along with circular patches of hide and flesh. Some investigators have suggested that these cases are the work of a devil cult gathering material for some bizarre rituals. Other investigators interpret the whole thing as the work of extraterrestrial specimen collectors, and they back up their theory with the numerous reports of UFOs that have been seen around the areas prior to the events.

Even so, if we are allowed to apply the theories of the columns or vortices of swirling energy to these cases, it can be shown that they fit the phenomenon very nicely.

To begin with, the evidence found at these sites suggests that the animals were on their feet at the beginning of the "attack" and that most of the mutilation occurs on the underside of the animals. If a highly energetic column or vortex were to erupt from the earth directly under the animals, then we might expect some rather startling effects. Being electrical in nature—as suggested by Persinger and others—and also capable of weakening the nuclear binding forces—as proposed by Wilbert Smith—then the combination might literally disintegrate the animals' hides and flesh on contact, obliterating the genitals or udders along the way. If the rising energy continued its upward surge and became entrapped inside the animal's body, it would expand trying to escape, possibly exiting through rectum or throat, taking with it muscles, tongue, and other vital parts.

Another curious fact about these mutilations is the appearance of surgical skill in the removal of hide or other parts. There are never any knife marks, and not a drop of blood is ever spilled. This has prompted some theorists to suggest that the work was done by an expert using a laser knife. The energy in an erupting vortex, however, could make a laserlike cut under certain conditions, and the blood might be congealed or evaporated.

In the majority of these cases the animals appear to have been transported away from the areas where they are normally confined. This, along with the fact that no tracks or footprints are ever found in the area, has led some to assume that the animals were abducted by aliens in UFOs or cultists in helicopters. Instead the animals might simply have been levitated by forces in the vortex that nullify gravity in the same way proposed for the levitation of rocks or other materials.

In mid-June 1976, a mutilation case that occurred on a farm located near Dulce, New Mexico, provided Officer Gabe

Valdez of the New Mexico State Police with some strange clues. Evidence found near the site of the mutilation revealed that the cow had been picked up and dropped to the ground at 150-foot intervals three times before the carcass was left on the ground. All around the carcass were a series of depressions, and these went off in a straight line fifty degrees to the right of the original course, leaving a trail of rounded depressions, approximately five inches across and three inches deep, spaced at exactly twenty-eight-inch intervals. These went on for a distance of five hundred feet and ended at a typical UFO landing site complete with burn ring and depressions in a triangular pattern.

So far no aliens have been caught, nor have any cultists. But the mutilations are continuing.

While much is already known about electricity and its actions, relatively little is known of what electricity actually is. On top of this there is much to be learned about sudden reversals of high voltage. Add to this the theories offered here and electrical energy becomes even more of a mystery than all of the unexplained events combined.

While qualified scientists spend years trying to uncover the answers to these questions, even greater puzzles are being added to the list. Photographs in the files of UFO groups such as APRO (Aerial Phenomena Research Organization), MUFON, and others show what appears to be light-absorbing UFOs, light-radiating UFOs, and UFOs that appear to be actual solid, metallic craft. This in itself suggests that the phenomenon is made up of more than one component. It is as if there are UFOs directly related to the forces from the earth and the forces from another planet or dimension. Add to this the fact that there is a considerable amount of evidence to suggest that a portion of the UFO phenomenon is linked to psychic forces. This may have something to do with the electrical or electromagnetic properties that link some UFOs with vortices of energy. Evidence already exists from laboratory experiments to show that certain radiations can induce unconsciousness or paralysis. If such states can be produced in experiments, then the same thing may happen to humans who come too close to an energetic column or vortex that is creating a luminous glow or UFO. The fields around these would be saturated with energy vibrating at various rates. Some of these may be found to be capable of triggering psychic states in those caught within the fields. Like rapture zones, they might ensnare individuals and involve them in experiences once known only to the tribal shaman.

If the energies in the columns are the result of stress in the rock structures of the earth (brought on by shifting pressures), then it would be interesting to know the parameters involved. How much energy, for instance, would be radiated into the atmosphere from one particular rock surface if an enormous weight of stone was stacked on it, as in the case of the Great Pyramid of Cheops in Egypt? Was this the secret behind this and similar structures? Did the massive weight produce stress in the rock base that provided a curtain of energy around the structure and allowed contact with the spirits, as in the shaking tent?

The answers to these and other questions may one day solve the mysteries behind the strange events that have plagued the Great Lakes for centuries. We can only wait and see. But while we wait, the region around Lake Ontario will continue to spew out its invisible forces.

# Bibliography

*All Around the World.* First Series, Glasgow: William Collins, Sons & Co., 1868.

Bowen, David I. *Shipwrecks of the Great Lakes.* Quebec: R. E. Publishing, 1969.

Boyer, Dwight. *Strange Adventures of the Great Lakes.* New York: Dodd Mead, 1974.

Cayce, Edgar E. *Edgar Cayce on Atlantis.* New York: Warner Books, 1968.

Charroux, Robert. *The Mysterious Past.* New York: Berkley Medallion Books, 1975.

Copway, George. *Traditional History of the Ojibway Nation.* London: Charles Gilpin, 1850.

Dewdney, Selwyn, and Kidd, Kenneth E. *Indian Rock Paintings of the Great Lakes,* Toronto: University of Toronto Press, 1962.

Gourley, Jay. *The Great Lakes Triangle.* New York: Fawcett, 1977.

Karagulla, Shafica. *Breakthrough to Creativity.* Santa Monica: DeVorss, 1967.

Kilner, W. J. *The Aura.* New York: Samuel Weiser, Inc., 1973.

Lambert, R. S. *Exploring the Supernatural.* Toronto: McClelland & Stewart Ltd., 1966.

Mansfield, J. B. *History of the Great Lakes.* J. H. Beers & Co., 1899.

Metcalfe, W. *Canvas & Steam on Quinte Waters.* Picton, Ontario: Picton Gazette Publishing, 1968.

Mitchell, Edgar D. *Psychic Explorations.* New York: G. P. Putnam, 1974.

Murphy, R. W. *Ghosts of the Great Lakes, Inland Seas,* Vol. 17,

No. 2. Cleveland: Great Lakes Historical Society Journal.

Ontario Historical Society. *Papers & Records*, Vol. 5, Toronto, 1904.

Ostrander, Sheila, and Schroeder, Lynn. *Psychic Discoveries Behind the Iron Curtain*. Englewood Cliffs: Prentice-Hall, 1970.

Ross, Robertson J. *The Diary of Mrs. John Graves Simcoe*. Toronto: William Biggs, 1911.

*Royal Canadian Astronomical Society Journal*, 7-148; 7-405.

Rzhevsky V., and Novik, G. *The Physics of Rocks*. Moscow: Mir Publishers, 1971.

Scadding, H. *Toronto of Old*. Toronto: Oxford University Press, 1966.

Smith, W. B. *The New Science*. Ottawa: Keith Press, 1978.

Snider, C. H. J. "Schooner Days." Toronto: Toronto *Telegram* (files).

Vastokas, M. J., and Vastokas, R. K. *Sacred Art of the Algonkians*. Peterborough, Ontario: Mansard Press, 1973.

# Index